Henry Stevens

John Farley

PROPHETS OF THE CHRISTIAN FAITH.

Prophets of the
Christian Faith

BY

F. W. Farrar, D.D.,
W. H. Fremantle, D.D.,
A. M. Fairbairn, D.D.,
Marcus Dods, D.D.,
George Matheson, D.D.,
Adolf Harnack, Ph.D.,
T. T. Munger, D.D.,
Lyman Abbott, D.D.,
A. C. McGiffert, D.D.,
Francis Brown, D.D.,
A. V. G. Allen, D.D.

London:
JAMES CLARKE & CO., 13 & 14, FLEET ST.

1897.

CONTENTS.

I.

WHAT IS A PROPHET?

By the Rev.
LYMAN ABBOTT, D.D.

I.

WHAT IS A PROPHET?

"Just as a dumb or retired person," says Ewald, "must have a speaker to speak for him and declare his thoughts, so must God, who is dumb with respect to the mass of men, have His messenger or speaker; and hence the word [prophet], in its sacred sense, denotes him who speaks not of himself, but as commissioned by his God." Accepting this general definition, the prophet is an interpreter of God to men; he is not so much a foreteller as a forthteller. He receives his message from the Eternal and gives it as the messenger of the Eternal. The difference between the prophet and the priest is far more radical than Carlyle has represented it to be in his "Heroes and Hero-Worship." The priest interprets man to God. The office of priesthood assumes that God is too holy for ordinary mortals to approach; that some special persons must be appointed to mediate between

man and God and approach God in lieu of, or
in behalf of, man. He who believes that God
is the All-Father, and that His ear is open to
the faintest cry of His feeblest child, will have
no place in his thoughts for any such mediator
between man and his God. The office of the
prophet is quite different. The need of a
prophet grows, not out of the inaccessibility of
God, but out of the imperfection of men. It is
not—in this I venture to differ with Ewald, at
least in phraseology—because God is dumb, but
because man is deaf. Man lives so in the
sphere of the material, he is so dependent upon
the senses as a medium of communication, that
he cannot appreciate, cannot understand, can
hardly even receive, a message which is not
translated into words. He is, indeed, the
recipient of certain vague impressions, but he
cannot interpret their meaning. He requires
some one to interpret them to him, to embody
them in language, to explain himself to himself,
and so to make God and God's message clear to
him. There is something like this in literature,
art, and music. The poet, the artist, the
musician, are each a kind of prophet. In all
men there is some poetic nature, some dim

perception of truth and beauty felt rather than
perceived; sometimes it is not even felt, there
is only a potentiality of feeling. The poet, by
his expression, develops this potentiality, brings
forth this hidden and sub-conscious life into
consciousness, enables the soul to perceive what
it could not perceive without this poetic interpreter. So the artist awakens the dormant
sense of beauty, by presenting beauty to the
sense-perception of men who were incapable of
perceiving it by pure imagination; and the
musician evokes musical life in souls incapable
of responding to unheard music. Similarly, in
every soul there is a possibility of Divine life, a
half-conscious recognition of truth and duty, of
purity and love, of goodness and God. The
prophet utters what unprophetic souls only
vaguely feel, and thus vitalises their feeling and
converts it into will, purpose, action.

Prophecy, then, assumes that God is ever
brooding His children, awakening in them a life
higher than their own, leading them up into
life and light, as the sun leads up the plant
from the darkness of the soil into the light of
day. Some men are hardly conscious of this
Divine life; others are conscious of it only on

rare occasions; some possess it as a vague,
uninterpreted feeling, an enigmatical, restless
desire for they know not what, a dream from
which they seem to themselves to be continually
awakening to the stern realities of life, a half-
seen vision which disappears before it is really
discerned; while to some it is the dominant
force of their lives, the directing purpose, the
rudder-holding hand, the great reality. Among
these last, those who have the power to phrase
this Divine life in words, to interpret it so as to
make its meaning clear to their fellows, are the
world's prophets. They receive their message
from God, and give it to their fellow-men.

Thus the prophets interpret God to man.
But they also interpret man to himself. They
explain to him what was before enigmatical in
his own aspirations. They make legible the
before invisible writing in his own experience.
Every man is at times vaguely conscious of an
unknown tongue speaking within himself. The
prophets translate this unknown tongue. And
no less do they interpret the age to itself.
They see, not always, not generally, with
infallible accuracy, but more clearly than their
less spiritually-minded fellows, what is the

meaning of the age, what the providential
purpose which is in process of fulfilment, what
its Divine trend, what its great issues are sure to
be. And because the object of their speech is
to prepare men for these issues by interpreting
to them this providential purpose, their forthtelling is also a foretelling. The prophet is not
a mere historian; he is a historian only for the
purpose of interpretation, and an interpreter
only for the purpose of leadership. For his
purpose is always to lead the people forth, to
enable them to understand God's will in order
that they may do God's work.

The prophet, therefore, is always a combination of piety and sympathy. A recluse is never
truly a prophet. The mere man of action is
never truly a prophet. He must be both a man
of his time and a man of eternity. He is to
interpret God to the men of his age; he must,
therefore, understand both God and the men of
his age. He is to translate the language of
heaven into the language of earth; he must,
therefore, understand both languages. He must,
accordingly, first of all be what the Bible
calls him, a "man of God," that is, a
man whose life is born of God and comes

forth from God. He must walk with God,
live with God, commune with God, or he
cannot understand God's message. He must go
up into Mount Sinai with Moses, up into the
Mount of Transfiguration with Christ. He
must be at times absolutely alone with his God
to receive God's message. But it is not enough
that he receive the message; he must also be
able to impart it. Not every spiritually-minded
man is a prophet. He must also understand
men—the men of his own age—their lives, their
experiences, their needs. The prophets, therefore, belong to no class or order. Rarely has
one been taken from any select circle, whether
ecclesiastical or social. Moses was a herdsman,
David a shepherd, Isaiah a peasant's son.
When one is found in the hierarchy, this very
fact limits his usefulness; Ezekiel is not so
widely read nor so widely useful as the Great
Unknown. The school of the prophets produces
no prophets. They cannot be created by
educational processes. Education may add to
their equipment, but it is not and cannot be the
secret of their power. That lies in the possession
of this twofold faculty—the hearing ear and the
speaking mouth; the ear to hear God, the

mouth to speak to man; the understanding of
God's message, and the capacity to impart it to
men who have not understood it.

It is a mistake to suppose that the prophet is
always, or even generally, the bearer of a new
message to the world. This he may sometimes
be, but more generally he interprets to a wider
circle a truth before known only to a few; or
makes vital in life a truth which before was
only a philosophical opinion; or restores to
human consciousness a truth it had lost; or puts
into new and better perspective a truth which
had been suffered to lie forgotten in the background; or carries on to its legitimate and
necessary conclusions truths whose issue and
meaning the world had not seen; or makes
new applications of familiar truths. The few
philosophers of Egypt believed that there was
one God above all gods; Moses brought this
truth out of its hiding-place in the schools and
made it the foundation of a new State and the
inspiration of a new worship. This prophet of
the Law taught that God is one, that He is a
righteous God, and that He requires righteousness of His children. This is the burden of the
Book of the Covenant, which is probably the

oldest writing in the Bible, and of Deuteronomy,
which, whatever its date as a manuscript,
embodies the prophetic message of Moses, the
great Lawgiver. David brought into the foreground the truth that God is merciful, sang of
a Father who pities His children, and handed
down to future generations, as his bequest to
them, the revelation embodied in the phrase,
" The sure mercies of David." Elijah proclaimed nothing new; he simply retold the
story of the past—one God, just and merciful;
he was the prophet of a restoration. The Great
Unknown—the second Isaiah—himself taught
by the years of captivity in Babylon that the
spirit of righteousness and reverence is not confined within any geographical boundaries, saw
clearly that if there is but one God, ever
righteous and merciful, then His law extends
over all nations and His mercy is provided for
all; he was the prophet of a catholic religion.

It is equally a mistake to suppose that
prophecy ceased and prophets were no more
after the coming of Christ. It is true that a
chief message of the Old Testament prophets,
from Moses to Malachi, is that a Messiah is yet
to come; and, of course, after He had come,

this theme, as one of foretelling, ceased for ever.
What had been prophecy became history. The
Incarnation, which had been a vision and a hope,
became a fact witnessed to by the senses : a
somewhat concerning which the Apostle could
write, " which we have seen with our eyes,
which we have looked upon, and our hands
have handled of the Word of Life." But in
the larger sense of a forthtelling—a spiritual
perception, and an effective interpretation—
prophecy has not ceased, and will not, until
every eye shall see Him face to face. A wider
range of prophecy, not its cessation, is anticipated by Joel as the result of the Incarnation.
The secret of prophecy is imparted by Christ to
the Apostles when He breathes upon them ;
the promise of prophecy, when He promises the
Holy Spirit to guide them into all truth ; the
commission to prophesy, in the command,
" What ye hear in the ear, that proclaim ye
upon the housetops." Prophets are mentioned
in the Book of Acts as recognised teachers in
the Apostolic Church, and are included by Paul
in his list of its ministers ; and the preacher's
recipient faith is accounted by him as at once
the measure and the secret of the prophet's

forthtelling. To deny to the Christian Church prophets, to assume that prophecy ceased with the close of the New Testament canon, to draw a sharp line between the prophets before and the prophets subsequent to the first century, appears to me to foster two errors: one, that which imputes to the Hebrew prophets an infallibility which they never claimed for themselves; the other, to deny to the Church since Christ that presence of a living, speaking, interpreted God, which was characteristic of the Hebrew Church, and which Christ distinctly and emphatically declared should continue to be characteristic of the Christian Church.

In a true sense, every real preacher is a prophet. If he is not a prophet, if he does not receive a message direct from God which he can communicate to man, if he is not a forthteller, an interpreter, a Divine messenger, he is no true preacher. In one respect he has an immeasurable advantage which the earlier prophets did not possess. His message he can always compare with the life and teachings of his Master, and thus determine whether it is in very truth a Divine message or only a human phantasy. His message will sometimes, perhaps generally,

be a simple re-enunciation of that which other
Christian prophets have given or are giving;
but it will have no real prophetic power unless
it has come to him from his Father, for he can
prophesy only according to the proportion of
his faith, only as what he has heard in the ear
he is proclaiming from the pulpit. But while
thus every Christian preacher may be and
should be a prophet, an interpreter of the
mystic voice of God to the men of his generation, there have been pre-eminent prophets in
the Christian Church as there were in the
Hebrew Church, men whose message has had
all the force of a new revelation, men whose
faith vitalised truths that were before held
as mere inert opinions, or revived truths
that had been forgotten, or revealed—that
is, unveiled—truths to the common people
which had been concealed in the closets
of the few, or made new applications of
familiar truths to new and unfamiliar conditions of life. These men are as truly prophets,
interpreters, forthtellers, as Isaiah, Jeremiah,
or Ezekiel. Such was Clement of Alexandria,
with his message of the Divine immanence;
Augustine, with his message of Divine sover-

eignty from the authority of which no man can
escape ; Luther, with his message of personal
responsibility to God and therefore personal
freedom from all who interpose themselves
between the soul and God ; John Wesley, with
his message that the Christian religion is the
universal religion, adapted to all sorts and
conditions of men ; Jonathan Edwards, with his
revived statement of the combined messages of
Clement and Augustine, Divine sovereignty and
Divine indwelling ; Swedenborg, with his
message that religion is life, not ritual or
dogma ; Maurice, with his message of a living
God as the Father of whom the whole family in
heaven and on earth is named ; Bushnell, with
his message of the transcendent character of
spiritual experience and the inadequacy of all
creeds, traditions, and theologies to give
expression to it ; Channing, with his message
that man is God's son, however far he may have
wandered from his Father's house ; Finney,
with his message to a paralysed Church bound
in the chains of a fatalistic philosophy, " All
things are possible to him that believeth " ;
Henry Ward Beecher, with his message sum-
moning the Puritan Church from bowing awe-

stricken at the foot of Mount Sinai to clasp love-stricken the cross on Calvary; Phillips Brooks, with his message of the universal presence and grace of God and the abundance of life in and through His indwelling—these and many others have been true prophets of the Christian Church. Every such man seeing the need of humanity, receiving his message from God and giving it as God's interpreter to God's children—a son of man, but no less a son of God, sent by God to be a forthteller of God's Word, in whatever age or community he may live, however large or small his audience, however fresh or familiar his message, is a prophet of the living God.

II.

ISAIAH AS A PREACHER.

By the Rev.
FRANCIS BROWN, D.D.

II.

ISAIAH AS A PREACHER.

MUCH depends on our understanding the relation of the prophets to their own times. It is difficult for some good people to learn that this is of primary consequence—only less fundamental than their close relation to God. The importance they have for us rests very largely on the more direct importance they had for their own contemporaries. No intelligent person now supposes that prediction is all of prophecy, but many intelligent persons fail to perceive or to appreciate the fact that, in God's ordering, predictive prophecy is conditioned by the circumstances that attended its birth, and is designed to affect contemporary belief and life. The same thing is true of the moral and religious teachings of the prophets. The prophets were not moral philosophers nor systematic theologians. Neither the speculative nor the scientific spirit controlled them. They had

visions, but they were not visionaries; they
taught great truths, but they were not professors
of dogmatics.   They were men of intense
spiritual life, eager to influence the national
organism of which they themselves formed a
part—the men and women among whom they
moved, whose wants and sins they clearly saw.
They were not essayists nor theorisers. They
were preachers and interpreters.   From the
stern announcements of Amos and the passionate
pleadings of Hosea, down to the fierce joy of
Nahum over Nineveh's fall, the melancholy of
Jeremiah at his people's calamity, and the
encouragements and spiritual exhortations of
Haggai, Zechariah, and Malachi, they are all
men of their own people, with throbbing,
longing hearts. Even the apocalyptic prophets,
such as Ezekiel, Joel, and Daniel, make present
conditions their starting-point. It is this which,
humanly speaking, gives to their messages their
permanent vitality.   Conditions and circumstances change, but the living God and the
heart of man abide, and those who have ever
really interpreted the one to the other are the
preachers of all time.

As soon as we recognise the prophets as

children and servants of their own age, the study of that age and its various periods and experiences becomes imperative. We cannot understand them without knowing the character and needs of their people at the time when they spoke. The better we know these—the more minutely we learn the fitness of prophetic utterances to the exact situations that called them forth—the richer will these utterances become for us, not only as memorials of a past age, but also, and especially, as messages to ourselves.

No prophet illustrates all this better than that most gifted of the prophets, Isaiah. Isaiah was a man of great natural endowments, intensified and consecrated to the loftiest ends by his self-surrender to God. He had the intellectual grasp of a great statesman, and the fervid imagination of a great poet. He could make combinations and foresee consequences, and warn him who ventured upon devious ways; he could portray with sustained power, he could overwhelm with the outpourings of righteous indignation, he could pierce with irony, he could cheapen with ridicule, he could mourn over his self-destroying people, he could

sympathise with the downcast, he could rise to
heights of spiritual experience and anticipation.
All his gifts were in the service of his generation. He was absorbed in them, and in God's
dealings with them. The present was awful to
him because of its issues for them; the future
was gloomy because it held punishment for
their obstinacy, or bright because after the
purification was to come their glory and their
peace.

Fortunately for us, in the case of no other
prophet have we a better opportunity to learn
the concrete character of his thought, or study
the influences which shaped its expression.*
While our information is only to a slight degree
of a personal character, and while our knowledge
of the contemporary history is not equally full
at all points, we find that there were two crises
in the national life around which many of
Isaiah's most telling sermons group themselves
—the Syro-Ephraimistic war (B.C. 734 ff.), with

* Among recent writers in English on this subject may
be named Canon S. R. Driver, D.D., "Isaiah, His Life and
Times," 2d Ed., 1893; Professor George Adam Smith, D.D.,
"The Book of Isaiah," Vol. I., 1889; Canon T. K. Cheyne,
D.D., "Introduction to the Book of Isaiah," 1895; Pro-
fessor Maximilian Lindsay Kellner, "The Prophecies of
Isaiah: An Outline Study," 1895.

the Assyrian campaign under Tiglathpileser III.,
by which that war was terminated, and the
invasion of Sennacherib, B.C. 701. Lack of
exact chronological arrangement in our present
Isaian collection makes the assignment of the
various addresses and sermons more difficult
than it otherwise would be, but scholars are
fairly well agreed as to the illustrations here
given.

As so frequently happens under autocratic
rule, the humiliation of Judah under Ahaz
followed speedily upon the military successes
of Uzziah and Jotham—Ahaz's grandfather and
father. The bold leader and strong ruler passes
away, a weakling succeeds him, and there is no
habit of self-control, self-reliance, and responsible patriotism in the many, to take the place
of the one vigorous hand. Probably the earliest
words of Isaiah preserved to us are those in
which he characterised the moral condition of
Judah at the close of Jotham's reign and the
beginning of that of Ahaz, about the year 735.
Conquest had brought increase of wealth,
luxury, pride, idolatry, looseness of life, weaken-
ing of moral fibre. The inevitable consequences
of this emasculation could not be hidden from

the keen eye of Isaiah, divinely clarified, and
sweeping the horizon, upon which the might of
Assyria was distinctly looming up. Accusation
and warning have seldom been addressed to a
nation in nobler and more searching language
than that preserved to us—in a somewhat
fragmentary form, it is true—in Isa. ii. 6-21.
After the arraignment, vv. 6 ff., comes the
announcement of the judgment day of Yahweh,
vv. 12 ff.:

> For a day hath Yahweh Sebaoth
> Upon all that is exalted and high,
> And upon all that is uplifted,—yea it shall be
> laid low,—
> And upon all the cedars of Lebanon,
> And upon all the oaks of Bashan.
> And upon all the high mountains,
> And upon all the uplifted hills,
> And upon every tower that is lofty,
> And upon every fortified wall,
> And upon all Tarshish ships,
> And upon all the objects of delight,
> And the haughtiness of man shall be abased,
> And brought low the loftiness of men,
> And Yahweh alone shall be exalted
> In that day !

The early part of the third chapter contains
the prophet's scourging attack on the political

condition of the people under the weak and
effeminate rule of Ahaz.

For behold! the Lord, Yahweh Sebaoth,
Removeth from Jerusalem and from Judah
support and stay,
Hero and man of war, judge and prophet,
And diviner and elder, captain of fifty and exalted
one,
And counsellor and skilful magician and shrewd
enchanter,
And I will set boys as their princes, and children
shall rule over them (vv. 1-4).
My people, its overseer is a wilful child,
And women, they have ruled over it;
My people, those guiding thee are misleading,
And the way of thy paths they have swallowed
up (v. 12).

In the latter part of the same chapter comes
the intense and contemptuous ridicule of the
luxurious and worthless women of the court.
In chapter v., 8 ff., we find a group of " Woes "
pronounced upon oppression, intemperance, and
reckless presumption, and at the beginning of
the same chapter a statement of the whole case
of Yahweh against Israel, in which sternness is
joined with profound and tender sadness :

What was there more to do for my vineyard that
I did not in it ?

Why did I expect it to bear grape-clusters, and it bore worthless things?

Chapter vii., which begins in narrative form, shows us the invasion of Pekah and Rezin already in progress, and the prophet vainly endeavouring to awaken faith in God in the heart of the superficial and faint-hearted Ahaz, who appears already to have formed the plan of saving himself from the allied enemies, Aram and northern Israel, by throwing himself into the arms of Assyria, as related in 2 Kings xvi. All Isaiah's assurances are of no avail, not even his declaration that deliverance is so certain and will be so speedy that a child soon to be born shall by right receive the name "God-with-us," because the hand of God shall by that time already be manifest in the defeat of the foe. Ahaz is too timid and too far involved with Tiglathpileser to respond, and the prophet is compelled to pass in vv. 17 ff. to an announcement of the disaster that will follow upon the Assyrian alliance.

To a time a little later, when Assyria was already on the move, belongs the declaration of judgment upon the Northern Kingdom, ix. 8-21, winding up with the magnificent description of

the oncoming Assyrian host, v. 26-30, which has
become displaced:

And he hath lifted up a signal to the nations
afar, and hath hissed to him at the end of the
earth,
And behold, hastily, swiftly, he cometh!
None weary, and none stumbling among them,—
he slumbereth not and he sleepeth not.
And the girdle of his loins hath not been loosed,
and the thong of his sandals not broken!
Whose arrows are sharpened, and all his bows
bent;
The hoofs of his horses, like flint are they reckoned,
and his wheels like the whirlwind!
A roar he hath like the lion, he roareth like the
young lions,
And he growleth, and he seizeth prey, and he
carrieth it safe away, and there is none that de-
livereth,
And he growleth over them in that day, like the
growling of the sea,
And they look to earth, and lo, thick darkness,
and the light hath grown dark in its clouds!
[For all this his wrath has not turned back, and
still is his hand stretched forth!]

About the second great crisis of Jerusalem
during Isaiah's ministry, that caused by the
invasion of Sennacherib in 701, another set of
prophecies group themselves. In these, although

the people is not freed from blame for the
perils of the situation, especially in respect to
the false move of intrigue with Egypt, the
general tone is more cheerful, and the expect-
ancy of deliverance more absolute. This time
the King (Hezekiah) and the prophet were in
more substantial accord. The words of Isaiah
contained in 2 Kings xix. 6, 7, 20 ff. (=Isa.
xxxvii. 6, 7, 21 ff.), indicate the hopeful tenor
of what he then felt moved to say. From a
somewhat earlier year are chapters xxix., xxx.,
xxxi., xxxii. ; more nearly coincident in time
are the verses xiv. 1-14. For our purposes the
prophecy concerning Assyria, x. 5 ff., may be
cited. The point of view is different from
that of ix. 7 ff., v. 26 ff. Here the presumption and the punishment of Assyria is
set in the foreground, and assurance is given
to Jerusalem of rescue from this seemingly
invincible foe.

Ho, Asshur ! rod of mine anger ! yea, a staff in
their hand is my wrath !
Against a profane nation do I send him, and over
the people of my rage do I command him ;
To take spoil and seize booty, and to make them a
trampling, like mire in the streets.

But he, not so doth he devise, and his heart, not so doth it reckon.

For to destroy (is) in his heart, and to cut off nations, not a few.

For he saith, Are not my princes altogether kings? Is not Calno as Carchemish?

Or is not Hamath as Arpad, or is not Samaria as Damascus?

As my hand hath lighted upon the kingdoms of the no-gods,—and their images are more than in Jerusalem,—

Shall I not, as I have done to Samaria and her no-gods, so do to Jerusalem and her idols?

But Yahweh shall punish him for his presumption. The passage ends with the imaginative picture of the approach of the Assyrian army to Jerusalem from the north, and its sudden overthrow (vv. 28-34):

He hath come upon Ayyath, hath passed by Migron, at Michmash he storeth his baggage;

They have crossed the path, at Geba they have taken night-quarters.

Ramah trembleth, Gibeah of Saul hath fled.

Cry aloud, daughter of Gallim, give ear, Layisha, answer her, Anathoth!

Madmenah hath become a wanderer, the dwellers in Gebim have hurried off (their treasures).

This very day he is to halt in Nob, brandishing

his hand against the mountain of the daughter of
Zion ;

Behold, the Lord, Yahweh Sebaoth, loppeth off
the boughs with frightful crash,

And the high in stature are hewn down, and the
lofty, they shall be laid low ;

And he shall cut down the thickets of the forest
with iron, and Lebanon by a mighty one shall
fall !

There is space now for only a word about
the specific Messianic predictions ascribed to
Isaiah—those in which the expectation of a
great deliverance involves a future king to be
the great deliverer. These, too, are rooted,
more or less distinctly, in the present, and
their expression is framed for effect upon the
prophet's own contemporaries. Scholars generally hold that the most definite and stirring of
them all found its point of contact with the
national life in the devastation of north-east
Israel by Tiglathpileser III., in the invasion
of 734, which cost Pekah his throne and his
life. It was then that Isaiah, keenly feeling
the blow which had fallen upon the sister
kingdom, recognising, indeed, the divine mission of Assyria, but believing this to be only
temporary, and confident that the haughty

invader must be overthrown, despairing of any
leadership in that overthrow on the part of the
weak, timorous, and self-willed Ahaz, received
power to announce the birth of the child who
was to conquer all enemies, set his people free,
and secure them peace. All the world knows
the verses now, and gives them a comprehensive
and spiritual interpretation, but the political
conditions of Isaiah's time have left an indelible
mark upon them, and we can interpret them
largely because he compressed into them so
much intensity of patriotic feeling and so much
confidence of faith. I am speaking of the great
prediction of ix. 1-6, ending with the stanza
(vv. 4-6) :

Yea, every boot of the man that stampeth with
noise, and garment rolled in blood—
It shall be for burning,—fuel for fire.
For a child is born to us, a son is given to us,
and the dominion shall come upon his shoulder,
And his name shall be called Wonder of a Counsellor, God-hero, Possessor of Spoil, Prince of Peace!
For the increase of the dominion and for peace
without end, upon the throne of David and over
his kingdom,
Establishing it and sustaining it, by justice and by
righteousness, from now, even for ever !
The zeal of Yahweh Sebaoth will perform this.

This portrayal of Isaiah's prophetic work has been meagre enough. Into some regions of his thought it has not been possible even to enter. But the illustrations given are sufficient to establish his greatness—greatness as an artist and greatness as a preacher. His sermons are poems, in which poetic fire and skill are wholly genuine and wholly at the service of his moral integrity and his spiritual insight, so that through them God revealed His will to the men of Isaiah's time, and has revealed His will afresh to the successive generations since Isaiah died.

III.

THE APOSTLE PAUL.

By the Rev.
GEORGE MATHESON, D.D., F.R.S.E.

III.

THE APOSTLE PAUL.

THE figures of the New Testament are representative men; each stands for some phase of the soul. Matthew is the type of conservatism, "that it might be fulfilled." Mark is the symbol of present action, "straightway He commanded." Luke is the embodiment of human sympathy. John is the love of the ideal. Nathaniel is the child; Nicodemus is the student; Peter is the youth; Thomas is the reflective and somewhat careworn man. No portrait in this gallery is without its special significance.

What is Paul? It seems at first sight equivalent to asking "What is Shakespeare?" It appears as if the only word which would describe him is myriad-mindedness. And yet, to my mind, the remarkable feature about Paul is not variety but unity—not the diversity of his experiences, but the one thread which connects

them. If I were asked to state in a single
phrase what Paul represents, I would say, " The
pilgrim's progress." I would say that his life,
as indicated in the historical order of his epistles, describes the normal course through which
each Christian is to journey in his passage from
the scene of shadows into the happy land of
Beulah.

I say, " the *normal* course." But the point I
wish to emphasize is that to Paul himself it was
very abnormal. He was the initiator of that
which has since become chronic and habitual.
The course proposed for the Old Testament
pilgrims was the very opposite of that pre-
scribed for Paul. Theirs was a march from the
desert into the promised land; Paul's was a
progress from the promised land into the desert.
They began with the valley, passed up to the
plain, and ended on the height; he began with
the height, passed down to the plain, and ended
with the valley. They proceeded from law to
love; he descended from love to law. They set
up their ladder on the earth and tried to reach
the heavens; he fixed his ladder in the heavens
and tried to reach the earth.

It was not only from the men of the Old

Testament that Paul was thus distinguished ;
his experience was equally marked out from the
original Apostles—the men of transition between
the old and the new. These proceeded from the
human to the Divine. They gazed first on the
Christ of the flesh. They followed the steps of
the Son of Man from the cradle to the cross ;
when the crown came, their pilgrimage was
over. But Paul began with the crown. His
first sight of the Christ was the Christ glori-
fied. He knew the power of His resurrection
before he felt the fellowship of His sufferings.
His progress was a progress backward. He had
begun with the light of immortality ; he had to
retrace his steps to take up the life of time. It
was an abnormal experience, though it was to
become universal. He was the first of the new
régime, and for a while the only one. He says
he was " born out of due time." I understand
him to mean, not that he was born too late, but
that he was born too soon. He claimed to have
a vision of the Christian life which was above
his age, before his day, in advance of his contemporaries. He claimed to be the follower of
One whose progress had been from heaven to
earth, who had begun with the form of God and

ended with the form of a servant, who had
emptied Himself step by step into sympathy
with things beneath Him, and paused not, rested
not, until He had made the human Divine. The
progress of St. Paul was like that of his Master
—a progress downward.

He begins in the air—in the other world.
He has been caught up to meet his Lord, and
the earth disappears from his view. He sees
nothing but the second advent; he hears nothing but the last trump. All perspective has
vanished : the end is at the door. Christ is
coming ; in a little while He will be here. What
is this world to any man ? Before His descend-
ing shout of triumph its proudest pomps shall
melt away. Before the first gaze of the man of
Tarsus there floated the form of only one Christ
—the Christ of resurrection. The light which
smote him from heaven put out all the candles
of earth. Everything below that sun became a
thing of insignificance. The kingdoms of the
world and the glory of them vanished like
smoke. Their inhabitants became as grass-
hoppers, their events as waterdrops. The only
bells heard were the bells of the New Jerusalem,
and they summoned all men to a cathedral above.

Then there came a cloud; I know not when,
I know not how. I only know it was somewhere between the Thessalonians and the
Galatians. In his letter to Corinth he speaks
of it as a thorn; in his letter to Rome
he describes it as a warfare; both are introduced as retrospects of a dark, and to some
extent a surmounted, past. The cause of the
cloud I cannot tell; probably it was something
external. But the main point is that it was
something which made Paul feel himself less
ready for his change. The second advent
moves further off; the world looms nearer.
He finds that the light which fell upon him
at Damascus was like the deluge; it had only
covered the old world—not annihilated it.
There were two natures within him—Saul and
Paul. For the first time in his life he felt
thoroughly bad. What right had he to
struggle? Had he not tasted of the heavenly
gift; had he not seen the Lord? Where was
the blessedness he had known in Arabia?
Where was the joy with which he had written
to Thessalonica? Where was the exultation
with which he had been taken up to the third
heaven? What was this that had come to him

—this flesh lusting against the spirit, this law
in his members warring against the law of his
mind?   Was not this spiritual death?   The
strong soul of yesterday beat upon his breast
and cried, " O wretched man that I am ! "

Then came a new gleam of glory, and it
came, not from the third heaven, but from the
very mist into which Paul had wandered.   It
brought a great message to his soul.   It said :
Your seeming fall is a rise.   You are further
removed from death now than you were in your
hour of immediate vision.   The true sign of
spiritual life is spiritual dissatisfaction.   There
is nothing which justifies a man like his belief
in the existence of a beauty which he himself
cannot reach.

Paul has come a step down his ladder, which
means a step up his pilgrimage.   He has come
nearer to the earth.   He has passed from sight
to faith—from an ideal of perfect satisfaction
to an ideal which eludes him by its glory.   But
already another step was preparing.   What was
that glory in Christ which had hitherto eluded
him ?   It was love.   The moment Paul said,
" I believe in love," he had put out his foot for
a further step downward.   Hitherto, however

beautiful, his experience had been mainly personal. He had found rest to his own soul. But that is not the half of the Christian life. Paul's deepest Christianity was yet to come. He had begun with sight; his passage from the Thessalonians to the Galatians had been a passage from sight to faith; his passage from the Galatians to the Corinthians is a passage from faith to love. You say "it was a very short time in which to make such a transition." Yes; but the transitions of God's Spirit are, in their last result, almost momentary. I can well-nigh hear the very hour strike in which he passed over the line. The man who wrote the magnificent hymn of the thirteenth chapter of 1st Corinthians has made a leap; and when he touches the ground it is no longer the old ground, but a plane higher in God's sight, because lower in the sight of man.

Can you fail to observe that from this time onward the teaching of Paul takes another channel? It becomes less personal, more humanitarian. Even his view of predestination is to my mind the result of his new breadth, not of his old narrowness. He sees that a mother's love is always *predestinating* love. When a

---

mother foreknows that her child is about to
come into the world, even before its birth, she
conforms it to an image; she figures
to herself what she would like it to be.
That is, in my opinion, the metaphor which
glittered before the eyes of the great Apostle
when he proclaimed that the All-Father had
predestined His children " to be conformed to
the image of His Son." Divine Love, fore-
knowing that its children were about to be
born, ere ever they had a character, ere ever
they had a being, planned for them a destiny of
glory, figured them in the likeness of the most
beautiful thing it knew, and said within itself,
" I baptize them into the name of Jesus." Nay,
was not baptism into Christ's name itself simply
the predestination of love—the expression in
the heart of the Divine Parent of a great, an
unquenchable desire that the new convert should
rise to heights altogether unearthly, and attain
to nothing less than the image of the Son?

Paul has now reached what he himself calls
the glory of the cross. He had begun with the
crown—the sight of the Christ of resurrection.
He had passed from sight to faith—the vision
of an ideal which was beyond him, and

after which he must strive. He has now come from faith to love—the perception that others have an ideal as well as he. Has Paul now arrived at the terminus? No. He has reached the knowledge that the cross is the glory of God; but there is a step beyond even that—he must " rejoice in *hope* of the glory of God." Faith in Christ was the parent of love, because it was the belief in love; but Paul makes the further discovery that love is the parent of hope. He says, in so many words, that the reason why he is not ashamed to hope is that the love of God is shed abroad in his heart (Romans v. 5). He was of a spirit not naturally sanguine; I have heard him called a pessimist. In his Epistle to the Thessalonians his main hope for the world seems to have been that a Divine power is keeping things from being worse; and truly he was right. But when the enthusiasm of the cross burst upon him, hope had a deeper revelation to bring. We again hear the clock strike as he passes the line. He had spoken of justification by faith; he had called love " a more excellent way "; he was now to cry, " We are saved by *hope*." Love was the parent of hope. No doubt the parent

was greater than the child; yet the child was
indispensable to the support of the parent.
And, with this latest birth in the soul of Paul,
there comes a widening of his horizon. There
is nothing which tells such tales as a letter, and
often most in the things it does not say. Already
in the Epistle to the Romans we begin to catch
breezes—currents of air which apprise us that
there is an opening somewhere not far away.
As we advance beyond the boundaries of that
Epistle, the current freshens. He tells the
Philippians in express terms that the purpose of
God's heart was that every man in every place
should bend his knee in prayer. A few miles
more and we are out in the open, with the gusts
of the great sea around us. As we pass from
the coasts of Philippi we are in a new element
—an element of breadth, I had almost said of
secularism, an element which increases in
strength from the outpouring of the letter to
Ephesus, until those notes of pastoral counsel
which speak the last farewell.

What is this new element in Paul? I have
called it secularism; it would be more correct
to call it the extension of the sacred. Hitherto,
Paul had seen in Christ merely the head of a

body of members. But now he began to see more. Christ was the head of the Church, but was He not also head of the State—of all principalities and powers? Was not this magnificent Roman Empire, however unconsciously to itself, already the kingdom of God? Was not Cæsar as much the servant of Christ as *he* was, albeit he knew it not? Was this world a secular system at all? Was the distinction between Church and State a real one? Would not the fulness of time show that all things had been " gathered together in Christ " ? As he approached Rome, and as the spectacle of Roman unity swam before his eyes, he asked himself if Christ's kingdom would be less incorporative than this kingdom of man. He asked himself if this Roman unity was really the work of Cæsar, if it was not itself only a product of that Divine order which had arranged thrones and principalities and powers. So asking, so thinking, Paul stepped into the world again. He came back to the haunts from which his conversion had lifted him; he claimed them for Christ. He found the land of Beulah on the earthly side. For the second time in his life he preached the things which once had been

alien to him. Very beautiful to my mind is the
passage, Ephesians iii. 14 and 15, in which he
declares that the idea of family life is modelled
after the relationship of the Father in heaven.
Beautiful, because I think there was a time
when Paul would not have said it—a time of
storm and stress below, of dazzling light above,
when the radiance of the heavenly vision had
blinded him to earthly ties. Beautiful, too,
because it is no accidental utterance. It is the
keynote of his latest song. If his morning
carol is to the Christ of the heavens, his evening
lay is to the Christ of the home; if he begins
with love on the wing, he ends with love in the
nest. All his latest notes are of home.

I cannot better conclude than by placing side
by side Paul's earliest and latest ideals of
Christian joy—the one from his first letter, the
other almost from his last. He says to the
Thessalonians, "We shall be caught up together
in the clouds to meet the Lord in the air"; he
says to Titus, "The grace that bringeth salvation hath appeared unto all men, teaching to
live soberly, righteously, and godly, in this
present world." Do I say that at the close of
his pilgrimage he has found his first experience

to be untrue? No; rather for the first time has he discovered its real value. He has found that the advantage of going up is the new strength we get for coming down. The bird that at dawn sings in the uplands may be heard in the afternoon on the ledge of an office wall; but the song on the office wall has been learned in the uplands. Moses had the vision of Nebo before coming down to the common lot of men; but the vision of Nebo helped him to come down. Paul's first revelation was the sight of immortality, but the sight of immortality gave value to the earth; and he who began with the vision of the ascending Christ was bound sooner or later to recognise the possibilities of " this present world."

IV.

CLEMENT OF ALEXANDRIA.

By the Rev.
MARCUS DODS, D.D.

IV.

CLEMENT OF ALEXANDRIA.

Titus Flavius Clemens, commonly known as
Clement of Alexandria, may be accepted as
the representative of Greek Theology. In some
respects either Origen or Athanasius might
more suitably stand as its exponent, but
Clement has the advantage of being earlier
than either of these great theologians, and of
being Origen's teacher and predecessor as head
of the catechetical school of Alexandria. "He
stands in the same relation to those that came
after him that Augustine sustained to the Latin
theology of the Middle Ages, or Luther and
Calvin to the later Protestantism."

Of his personal history little is known. He
wrote in the reign of Severus (193-211 A.D.),
and the probability is that he was born in
Athens about the middle of the second century.
In quest of truth he travelled in Italy, Syria,
and Asia Minor, until finally he "caught the

true Sicilian bee," Pantænus in Alexandria.
In a year or two afterwards he was ordained a
presbyter of the Church, and succeeded Pantænus as Master of the catechetical school.
His residence in Alexandria undoubtedly had
a great influence, not only on the form of
his writings, but on his thought, and especially on his attitude towards philosophy.
In this magnificent, busy, and dissipated
city, every vice of heathenism and the most
sumptuous and seductive idolatrous worship
were daily obtruded on the notice of Clement. Everything that paganism had to
attract, to delude, to bind, was matter of
familiar observation to the man who was
destined to become, not only the most volu-
minous, but in many respects the most saga-
cious and convincing, of Christian apologists.

In Alexandria Clement had also opportunity
to acquire that learning which was essential to
qualify him to meet the mental condition of
religious inquirers in the second century. It
was at least as important to gain to the new
faith the philosophers and scholars of the
museum as the mechanics of the docks and
building-yards, or the warehouse porters. His

office as teacher of the Christian school exposed
him to the interrogation of all who had difficulties about the new religion. The cavils
which were concocted by the wits of the
museum, the theories whieh were broached in
the dining-hall of the professors, would naturally find their way to the ears of Clement.
And so he drew around the young plants which
were under his charge the hedge, as he calls it,
of a learning superior to that of the assailants.
Excepting Athenæus, probably no ancient
writer could be named who cites four hundred
authors, but a larger number than this must
measure the reading of Clement. This great
learning he used, not for display, but as a
missionary engine. His three great books,
the "Protreptikos," the "Paidagogos," and
the "Stromateis," written respectively for the
heathen, the catechumen, and the Christian
Gnostic, all bear witness to his zeal no less
than to his knowledge.

In the apologetic of Clement we become
aware that his conciliatory attitude is the
result not merely of geniality of disposition,
but of principle—the principle, to state it in
his own words, that "there is one river of

truth, but many streams fall into it on this side and on that." He believed that Philosophy had been in its measure a "schoolmaster" to the Greeks, as the Law had been to the Jews; and that even after the Advent it served as a preparatory training which might lead men to Christianity. By "philosophy," as he is careful to explain, he did not mean the teaching of any particular school, the Platonic, Aristotelian, or Epicurean, but whatever had been well said by any sect "which teaches righteousness along with science." As Justin had taught that the Logos had been the revealer of truth to the heathen philosophers, so Clement maintains that philosophy is God's gift to men "for the sake of those who not otherwise than by its means would abstain from what is evil."

This catholic tendency which is so marked a feature of the second century, was no doubt stimulated, if not wholly caused, by the universalism of the Empire. As Professor Allen says, "The necessity of enforcing one common method of legal procedure upon a variety of peoples, each with its own conception of justice and of its practical administration, gave rise to the comprehensive spirit of Roman law and the endeavour to ground it in the nature of a man. A similar necessity gave rise to similar efforts in the sphere of religious thought." The necessities of Clement's position also drove him to adopt his liberal views and methods. He expressly affirms that he felt himself impelled to become a Greek to the Greeks, and that in order to remove their difficulties he must first feel them, must recognise the truth they held before he could add to it, and must see their error from their own point of view. Never, on the other hand, does he allow it to be supposed that he considers philosophy to be a sufficient guide. Christ alone possesses the whole truth. There is only One who can perfectly satisfy, only One who can heal, purify, and restore to God.

In this teaching Clement is the type not only of one of the most remarkable phases of early Christianity, but he is the representative of a tendency or mental attitude which reappears in all ages of the history of Christendom. It would appear from unmistakable signs, in our own day, that the Church has not yet made up its mind to adopt Clement's theory of the relation of non-Christian religions and philosophies

to Christianity. The Bampton Lecturer for
1894 (Mr. Illingworth), speaking of the non-
Christian sacred books of the world, says:
" With all their imperfection and manifest in-
feriority, there is that in them which we can
well believe to have been a vehicle of Divine
teaching to the nations they addressed, and, if
so, to have been inspired, as their possessors
believed." And in confirmation of his statement he quotes Clement, who speaks to the
same effect : " Perchance philosophy was given
to the Greeks, directly and primarily, till the
Lord should call the Greeks." And again, "The
barbarian and Greek philosophy has torn off a
fragment, not from the mythology of Dionysus,
but from the theology of the Eternal Word."
Yet the man who has done more for India and
for Christianity in India than any other during
this generation has been severely taken to task
for pointing out that Hinduism has in it elements of good and a contribution to make to
the Church and to the world.

St. Paul's method of dealing with the heathen,
his addresses at Lystra and at Athens, should
have made it impossible to deny that God has
been training Gentile as well as Jew for Christ.

And probably the idea that heathenism and all
its works are wholly of the devil is pretty well
obsolete. But there is still prevalent a lurking
fear that in recognising the good that is outside
Christianity the supremacy and essential distinction of our religion may be lost. Instead of
levelling up, a process of levelling down may
be initiated. And even although this fear must
not be allowed to blind us to the education of
the world as a whole, and to the part played by
the various races in that education, yet there
are undoubtedly dangers to be avoided. For
example, we see that in Clement this approxi-
mation of Christianity to philosophy caused
him all but uniformly to present Christ as a
teacher. With him redemption is little more
than the reception of Christ's teaching, the soul
being purified and, in the Platonic sense,
redeemed by the truth. Faith comes to be
nothing more than the mental acceptance of
the revelation of Christ. The saving power
of Christ consists in His manifestation of the
Father's love. The idea of a redemption by
expiation is quite in the background, and may
easily be overlooked. Christ saves by the
light He brings. Atonement is effected, not by

altering the relation of God to man, but by disclosing the actual relation and attitude of the Father towards His erring children. All who now hold that our redemption is accomlished by the knowledge of God which Christ brings may claim Clement as their theological ancestor.

The doctrines in which Clement's characteristic thinking most conspicuously emerges are his teaching about God, man, punishment, and the higher or Gnostic life. In his doctrine of God Clement followed the teaching of his philosophical progenitors, Plato and Philo. And, indeed, the whole trend of belief in the second century was towards the transcendence of God. The impossibility of His holding any direct living relationship with the world was freely taught by the Gnostics. And, in opposing Gnosticism, Clement did not repudiate the idea which lay at its root, although he evaded its consequences. With him God is the Absolute, the Monad. You cannot apply to Him the terms genus, difference, species, atom, number, accident, subject, whole, part, figure; nor can any name be properly or essentially given Him. But while thus exhausting language to empha-

size the remoteness and incomprehensibility of
God, Clement yet believed in His immanence.
All things and persons are penetrated by the
Divine Logos, the Son who is the consciousness
of the Father. Through the Logos God has
dwelt with men, has guided and educated the
race, has been, in all ages and races, anticipating
the Incarnation.

The Gnostics believed in a God who was
good but not just. Accordingly Clement
devotes a part of his "Paidagogos" to demon-
strate that goodness and justice are not incompatible. "The justice of God is good, and His
goodness just." And, hence, instead of holding
with the Gnostics that punishment was the
work of a subordinate and evil God, Clement
holds that all punishment is remedial and for
the sake of the punished. In this also he
followed Plato, but, as Dr. Bigg has clearly
shown, unadvisedly; for, whereas Plato held
that sin is the result of ignorance and is therefore a disease, Clement held that sin is the
product of will. If sin is a disease, punishment
may be remedial. But if sin is, as the Alexan-
drines held it to be, rebellion against God and
against Law, the case is altered. "Punishment

is the safeguard of Law, that is to say, of the
unity, life, and welfare of the whole, and of
the individual in and through the whole. It does
not aim at amendment, but at the maintenance
of that Law, which alone can amend." On
Clement's theory of punishment, also, it is
difficult to find the full significance of the
death of Christ, or even to perceive its
necessity.

In the characteristics of Clement's theology
now indicated many Christians of our own time
will find their prototype and legitimisation, but
it will be less obvious where contemporary
analogies are to be found for the teaching
which was most peculiar to him, his inculcation
of a lower and higher grade of Christian life.
No doubt we everywhere find that practically
Christians are divided into those who take their
Christianity seriously and those who do not, and
we also find some popular forms of teaching
which might be construed into a belief that
there are lesser and greater mysteries into which
Christians can be initiated. But in Clement we
find the distinction between the ordinary believer and the Gnostic or advanced Christian
elaborated and formulated. He believes the

distinction to be justified by St. Paul's distinction between the babes who require to be
fed with milk and the adult or spiritual who
can use solid food. The Gnostic is distinguished
from the common believer by many characteristics; he acts from the principle of love, the
common believer from fear or hope. The perfection of the former consists in doing good, of
the latter in abstinence from evil. The Gnostic
prays only in thought; his excellence consists,
not in controlling his desires and wishes and
passions, but in not having them; in him the
struggle between inclination and the sense of
duty is past. The Gnostic is a king; nay, he
becomes a god. His appellation of "Gnostic"
is justified by Clement's theory that "knowledge is superior to faith," that "through knowledge faith is perfected, as through it alone the
believer becomes perfect." "Faith is a com-
pendious knowledge of things which are of
urgent necessity; knowledge, a firm and valid
demonstration of things received through faith."
The final state of the Gnostic is perpetual contemplation of God. "The Gnostic soul, in the
grandeur of contemplation, embraces not the
Divine in a mirror or through a glass, but feasts

eternally upon the vision in all its clearness—
that vision with which the soul, smitten with
boundless love, can never be satiated — and
enjoys inexhaustible gladness for endless ages,
honoured by a permanent continuance in all
excellence."

Here, it will be obvious, we have a strange
combination of Paulinism, Gnosticism, Mysticism, and Stoicism. The relief and quickening
which Stoicism brought to many of the truest
souls in the Roman world proves that it does,
in a large if not in a perfect measure, satisfy
human instincts and cravings. Mysticism bap-
tizes it without enforcing that element in
Christianity which sanctifies work and commonplace people. That a state of absolute
superiority to pleasure and pain can be reached,
that this condition of "apathy" can be attained
by the contemplation of God, and that this is
the perfect bliss and eternal state of the soul—
these are the main contentions of Mysticism.
The superiority of the Gnostic to the common
believer is the very point which Bossuet saw to
be the foundation of all Madame Guyon's error.
"The doctrines which you advance, Madame,
involve the fact of an inward experience above

the common experience of Christians." But anything which even seems to throw a slight on the Christianity of the uneducated and toiling millions, or of the men who spend themselves in active efforts for the promotion of Christ's kingdom, is earnestly to be deprecated. Indeed, we have a personal interest in maintaining the sufficiency of the lower Christian life; for, as Dr. Bigg appositely remarks: "To most of us probably Miss Rossetti's words go home:

" We are of those who tremble at Thy Word,
    Who faltering walk in darkness towards our close
Of mortal life, by terrors curbed and spurred—
        We are of those.

" Not ours the heart Thy loftiest love hath stirred,
    Not such as we Thy lily and Thy rose,
Yet, Hope of those who hope with hope deferred—
        We are of those."

V.

ST. AUGUSTINE AS A PROPHET.

By the Rev.

ARTHUR C. McGIFFERT, D.D.,

Professor of Church History in Union Theological Seminary.

V.

ST. AUGUSTINE AS A PROPHET.

EVERY true prophet looks both forward and backward—is at once parent of the future and child of the past. Only as his life draws its nourishment from the world in which he lives, with all its heritage of bygone ages, can he stamp himself upon his own generation and mould the life of generations yet to come. Not one in the world's long line of "speakers for God" whose Divine message has not borne the imprint of earthly traditions and conditions— often of the organs at whose reformation or eradication that message was aimed! Indeed, the influence of every such prophet has been measured always, not alone by the Divine truth which he has lived and spoken, but also by the degree to which the thought and feeling of his fellows have found utterance in him. He has spoken, not simply to his age, but for it, if he has spoken with power and effect. It should,

therefore, not cause surprise if in the thinking
and teaching of Augustine, who for fourteen
centuries has influenced where he has not
dominated the thought of Western Christendom, there should voice themselves along with
his own peculiar message the prevailing tendencies of his time. It is hardly just to hold
him responsible for all that he received from
his age as well as for all that he gave it, and
it is curiously unhistoric to overlook, as is often
done, that which was truly his own, and to
stamp with his name that alone which was the
common property of his day and generation.

Augustine was born and bred in the midst of
an environment distinctly Roman in its character, and he knew Christianity before his conversion chiefly, if not solely, in that peculiarly
Latin form which it had acquired already more
than a century before, and which is nowhere
more clearly portrayed than in the writings of
his own countrymen, the lawyer Tertullian and
the ecclesiastic Cyprian. In that Christianity
the most characteristic feature was the domi-
nance of legalism. The Gospel was regarded as a
law or a collection of laws, by the observance of
which a man could gain eternal life, but the

disregard of which entailed eternal condemnation. God was conceived commonly under the aspect of Lawgiver and Judge, whose chief function was to reward men for obeying and to punish them for disobeying His commands. Faith still had a place as the initial act of the Christian life, and God's grace was still exercised through the " sacrament of regeneration " for the remission of sins committed before baptism; but for the Christian who sinned after receiving the cleansing rite there was nothing to depend upon but his own endeavours, divided between the attempt to obey and the effort to atone by works of penance for his daily acts of disobedience. The Christian life had thus become largely a mere matter of calculation. Not the overflow of the heart in love and gratitude to God ; not the instinctive striving of the soul after higher and better things for their own sake; but the payment of enough, and no more than enough, to insure escape from death and the enjoyment of the promised reward.

Naturally associated with such a conception of the Christian life was the tendency to push God ever further and further away—to lose all sense of communion with Him—to regard Him as a Tyrant to be feared and appeased rather than as a Father to be loved. It would carry us too far afield to trace the rise and development of this conception of God in Christian thought, but the resemblance between it and the God idea in Latin paganism is striking, and the predilection for it of the native Roman mind is unmistakable.

The same legalistic tendency which operated thus to degrade the Christian life and the Christian's God resulted also in the transformation of the primitive Christian brotherhood into the Holy Catholic Church of the third and following centuries. That which had been originally a mere communion of saints, bound together by a common faith and a common hope, had become already at an early day a great and thoroughly organised institution with its apostolic episcopate and its clerical sacerdotalism—an institution claiming to be the sole representative of Divine authority, rebellion against which meant rebellion against God Himself, and claiming to be the sole channel of Divine grace, outside whose pale salvation was impossible. It was to such a Christianity, embodied in such a Church, that Augustine was converted, under the preaching of the great Bishop Ambrose of Milan, and it is in the light of this environment that his Christian life and teaching must be studied. That he was affected by it and that much of his thinking bears its impress, that he showed himself, indeed, in his controversies with heretics and schismatics, a devout believer not only in the authority of the Church and in its right to demand implicit obedience both in thought and deed, but also in its exclusive privilege to dispense the saving grace of God, cannot be denied; and that he helped thereby to fasten upon the neck of Western Christendom the yoke of ecclesiasticism and sacramentarianism is doubtless true, but it is not this side of his teaching that is truly characteristic of him. It is not in what he received from his age, but in what he gave it, that his real significance lies. He had been no prophet had he simply voiced the thinking of his day. It was because he had another message to utter—a message received direct from God—that his name still lives beside the names of Paul and Luther.

"Thou movest us to delight in praising Thee;

for Thou hast formed us for Thyself, and our heart is restless till it rests in Thee." "I could not exist at all, O my God, unless Thou wert in me. Or should I not rather say that I could not exist unless I were in Thee, from whom are all things, by whom are all things, in whom are all things?" "O Thou strength of my soul, enter into it and prepare it for Thyself, that Thou mayest have and hold it without spot or wrinkle." "I call Thee into my soul, which, by the desire that Thou inspirest in it, Thou preparest for Thy reception." "Thou, Lord, hast blotted out all my evil deserts that Thou mightst not repay into my hands wherewith I have fallen from Thee, and Thou hast anticipated all my good deserts that Thou mightst repay into Thy hands wherewith Thou madest me." "I can do all things through Him which strengtheneth me. Strengthen Thou me that I may be able. Give what Thou commandest, and command what Thou wilt." "Another have I heard entreating that he might receive . . . by which it appeareth, O my holy God, that Thou givest when that Thou commandest to be done is done."

It is in such utterances as these, selected almost at random from his " Confessions," that the true Augustine speaks. His response to his contemporaries' low and unchristian conception of God is the abiding love of God, which leads Him to give all to man, who deserves nothing; the constant nearness of God, which makes intimate communion with Him always a possibility; the Fatherhood of God, which makes an unbroken fellowship with Him the supreme delight of the soul. His response to his contemporaries' commercial notions of the Christian life is the allness of God and the nothingness of man; the assertion that all that is good comes from God, and God alone; that man is good only in so far as he depends upon God and cleaves to Him; that no man can put God in his debt or establish a claim of merit over against Him, for there is no merit except God's merit, and to be independent of God is to be only evil. For an explanation of Augustine's thought of God and of man's relation to Him we may look in the Psalms and in the Epistles of Paul, which were his very meat and drink, and which he understood and appreciated as no one else in the ancient Church; or we

may look in Neo-Platonism, which profoundly
influenced him at a critical period in his career,
and which constituted for him a bridge from
scepticism to the Catholic faith. With its conception of Deity as the only true existence, and
of absorption in the Divine as the only true
good, it doubtless did much to mould his
thought. But though we may acknowledge
Augustine's indebtedness to these and other
influences, we must recognise the fact that his
theology, like his piety, finds his ultimate
ground only in his profound religious nature
and in his vivid experience. His was a nature
to which the Divine was as necessary as the air
he breathed, a nature open on its upward side
towards the infinities, and finding no satisfaction in aught that failed to breathe their inspiration. Even had he never known Christianity
he must have sought and remained unsatisfied
until he found Deity, for he was impelled God-
ward by the deepest craving of his soul.
" Thou hast formed us for Thyself, and our heart
is restless till it rests in Thee," is the cry, not
alone of Augustine the Christian, but of Augustine the man; and Christianity was what it
was to him, not, as to so many others, because

it promised him escape from punishment or the
enjoyment of reward, but because it opened
to him a vision of the God he had been seeking, because speaking in and through it he
heard and recognised God's voice. He was the
prophet, not of a distant God, but of a God
within man; not of a God who has withdrawn
and hidden Himself from His creatures, but of
a God who still reveals Himself to those who will
but open their eyes and look upon Him. He
was the prophet of such a God, and he prophesied whereof he knew. He spoke to his fellows
out of the fulness of a God-knowledge gained
by direct and intimate communion with Him.
He bore witness to what he had himself seen in
his immediate visions of the Father's face.
The secret of his marvellous influence over his
own and subsequent generations lies largely in
this very fact, that he prophesied, not of what
he had heard or thought, but of what he had
experienced—that he uttered not merely his
ideas, but himself. Divine truth was incorporated into his life before it found its way
to his lips; he lived his theology before he
taught it.

The dogma of original sin, for instance,

which Augustine asserted so strenuously in
his controversy with the Pelagians, and which
has brought such widespread disrepute upon
him, was no scholastic or artificial thing; it
was in the truest sense the fruit of his own
experience; nor was it out of line with his
highest thought of God and man. The more
vividly conscious he was of the presence of
the Divine, the more certain did he become of
the essential kinship between God and man—
a kinship which made necessary some thoroughgoing explanation of humanity's all-too-patent
lack of present oneness with Deity, in disposition and in sympathy. His insistence upon
the dogma bears witness to the strength of
his conviction that man was made for God
and finds his true life only in Him, and to
the keenness of his experience of the empty
and unsatisfying character of man's ordinary
life, compared with the possibilities of a life
of unbroken converse with the Divine. And
so the doctrine of unconditional predestination,
upon which he also laid such earnest stress,
rooted itself, not in any artificial conception
of God and of man's relation to Him, but in
the experimental knowledge that God alone is

good and the source of good, and that there
is no such thing as independent, self-originated
human merit. However harshly this truth
may have found expression in the controversies in which Augustine was engaged—however narrowly and artificially it may have been
interpreted at times by Augustine himself—
however unwarrantably it may have been made
to justify extreme and erroneous conceptions of
man and of God's dealings with him, the utterance of such a truth must have stamped Augustine as a true prophet of God in whatever age
and under whatever circumstances he had
spoken. The utterance of it in an age per-
meated with the belief that man and God
have nothing in common, and that God blesses
only the man whose independent, self-originated merit makes him rightfully God's cred-
itor, stamps him as one of the very greatest of
all God's prophets. His was indeed the voice
of one crying in the wilderness—proclaiming
to his fellows the message which Christ Himself had uttered when He revealed God in
human form, and thus disclosed the true
source of all that is truly good in man.

Augustine has often been accused of giving

currency, especially through his " Confessions,"
to an unhealthful mysticism which inevitably
leads to quietism and saps the energy of the
Christian life.   There was undoubtedly an
element of mysticism in Augustine's piety—
as in that of all the world's great religious
geniuses—but his mysticism was not that
of the East, and the pantheistic mysticism
which was so widespread in the West during
the later Middle Ages had its progenitor not
in Augustine but in the Neo-Platonism of
Pseudo-Dionysius.   Genuine Latin that he
was, Augustine dealt in terms of personality
rather than in terms of nature, and it was
not of a physical union between Deity and
humanity that he thought, but of a personal
union between God and man.   It is a fact of
great significance that it was not through his
study of the universe, but through his study
of himself that his eyes were at length opened
to the God he had so long been seeking.   " God
and the soul—that is what I desire to know,"
he says in his Soliloquies.   " Nothing more ?
nothing whatever."

He was a psychologist before he was a
theologian, and his apprehension of his own

individuality was far too vivid to permit him to
content himself in genuine mystic fashion with
the idea of a mere absorption in Deity as the
end of existence, while his acquaintance with
the innermost workings of his own soul was
too thoroughgoing for him to conceive of any
union between God and man which was not
conditioned primarily upon a conscious unity
of will and purpose. And so he found, not
in mere contact of nature with nature, whether
through mystic contemplation or through participation in the sacrament of the body and
blood of incarnate Deity, but in the love of
the human heart for God, the true secret of
oneness with Him. This was the Christianity
which he preached : the heart of man responding to the heart of God—love answering love
—self lost, not in the contemplation of Deity,
but in devotion to Him. Truly, motive power
enough in such teaching to transform the life
of Christendom !

Augustine did not live in vain. It is true
that many of the traditional misconceptions
which his higher views should have led him
to repudiate find expression in his writings,
and that much that is artificial and unhealth-

ful in Christianity has in his teachings a war-
rant for its existence; but, in spite of the fact
that he was a child of his age and was unable
to free himself completely from its bondage, he
gave to those who came after him a conviction
of the abiding grace of God and of man's constant dependence upon him which had in it the
seeds of better things to come. This very conviction might, as it did in subsequent generations, bind the yoke of ecclesiasticism even
more tightly upon the neck of Christendom by
magnifying the need of that grace which the
Church alone could dispense; but in spite of
the evil consequences which flowed from such a
tendency, Augustine's conception of God was
and remained a blessing. God a Father instead of a mere Avenger, even if the Father
only of those within the Catholic Church;
God near instead of far, even if near only in
the sacraments: this was no small gain; and
there came a time when the great truth uttered
by Augustine found a clearer-eyed and surer-
voiced champion in Augustine's greater disciple,
Luther. Their Gospel was one, but eleven centuries of ecclesiasticism and sacramentarianism
had taught the later prophet what the earlier

had not learned. The evangelicism of the great Reformation of the sixteenth century was Augustine's, its Protestantism was Luther's own.

VI.

JOHN WYCLIFFE.

By the Very Rev.
W. H. FREMANTLE, D.D.

JOHN WYCLIFFE.

WYCLIFFE was a prophet. We must not
limit the spirit of prophecy to the Old Testament. Not only do we read of prophets in
New Testament times at Antioch (Acts xiii.
1) and Corinth (1 Cor. xii. 28), but also in
the ancient writing called the "Didache" and
in the hymn "Te Deum." Why should we
confine prophecy to those first Christian ages?
On the tomb of Luther the inscription rightly
stands, "Propheta Germaniæ."

The special character of the prophet is that
of one who speaks for God; and of one who
does this, not as a scribe who reads from a
book, nor as an ordinary pastor who makes use
of all the means at hand to influence men, but
as one in direct communion with the Unseen.
And, further, the prophet's message is always
one of Righteousness. He disentangles God's
righteousness from the wrappings of system,

and makes it stand out bright and burning
before the eyes of men.

But there are differences in the form which
the message takes, and the medium through
which it operates. Carlyle presents to us the
Hero in different guises—as Priest, as Statesman, as Man of Letters. We may do the same
with the Prophets. In Wycliffe we may see
the Prophet as Schoolman. The Schoolmen,
too, had their different titles. Aquinas was
the Angelic, Bonaventura the Seraphic, Ockham the Invincible or the Singular. Wycliffe
was the Evangelical Doctor. The Evangelical
Righteousness which filled his soul is the key to
all his thought and teaching. It led him, first,
to maintain the Scriptures as supreme above
traditions, Fathers, councils, Papal decrees;
secondly, to uphold the rights of the nation, as
the organ of public righteousness, against the
Pope and the clergy; thirdly, to insist on the
paramount importance of the pastoral office over
the work of the monastic orders; and, lastly,
to rehandle the doctrine of the Church in the
light of Scripture and of sound reason. All
this makes him to be justly esteemed as the
pioneer, or Morning Star, of the Reformation.

Wycliffe was born about 1320, at Spresswell,
near Old Richmond on the Tees, in the north
of Yorkshire, close to the village of Wycliffe,
from which his family took its name. But,
like other prophets, he was without honour in
his own house; his family were, and remained,
strong Papists. Of his early training we know
nothing; he probably went to Oxford about
the age of fifteen, and became a scholar and
afterwards a Fellow of Balliol College. This
College, which had been founded by John of
Balliol in 1262 and consolidated by his widow
Dervorquilla in 1282, was connected with
Wycliffe's country through the endowments
which they had given it (and which it still
possesses) at Bernard Castle on the Tees, and
was the rallying-place for the "Boreales" or
Northern men, as Merton College was for the
Southerners.

The colleges at Oxford were at first little
more than lodging-houses where poor scholars
were provided for while they were reading for
the higher degrees. When Wycliffe joined
the University there were, in the College
which has attained in our day a leading
academical and social position, twenty-two

Fellows, with a weekly allowance of eight farthings apiece for maintenance; they were bound to resign when they took the degree of Master of Arts, and their Master was elected from among themselves. Their position was improved in 1341 by the benefactions of Sir William Felton and Sir Philip Somerville, through which their allowance was increased to twelve farthings a week (equal to about five shillings now), with clothing; six Theological Fellowships were instituted; and the Fellows were allowed to remain till they should attain a sufficient living from the Church. Since the rule still remained that the Master must be elected from among the Fellows, it is all but certain that Wycliffe held one of these Fellowships till he was made Master, about the year 1358.

In 1361 Wycliffe was appointed Rector of Fillingham, in Norfolk; in 1369 he changed this benefice for that of Ludgershall, in Bucks, some ten miles from Oxford; and in 1374 he was appointed by the Crown to be Rector of Lutterworth, which position he held till his death in 1384. At the first of these parishes he seems to have seldom resided; the leave of

absence which he craved in 1368 from the
Bishop of Norwich in a still extant petition,
in order that he might devote himself to study
at Oxford, probably denotes his usual practice,
a practice common in that and many other
times; at Ludgershall, as being nearer to
Oxford, he was probably more constantly
resident, and at Lutterworth he fully dis-
charged the pastoral duties. His increased
sense of responsibility and of the importance
of the pastoral office no doubt made him
unwilling to hold the cure of souls as a mere
benefice. Yet he was often in Oxford, even
till his last years; he appears to have had
some connection with Queen's College, where
his name occurs as occupying a room.

His studies began with what was called the
Trivium—Grammar, Dialectics, and Rhetoric;
and the Quadrivium—Arithmetic, Geometry,
Astronomy, and Music. But there is evidence that he studied with enthusiasm Natural
Science and Natural History; and he became
thoroughly versed in legal studies, not only in
the Canon and Civil Law, to which he would
necessarily be led by theology and Church
history, but also the laws of England. Oxford

was at that time the most celebrated university
in Europe. It had produced within one hun-
dred years Roger Bacon, the physicist (the
Doctor Mirabilis, d. 1292); Grostete, the just
and patriotic Bishop of Lincoln (d. 1253);
Duns Scotus, the Realist (d. 1308); William of
Ockham, the Nominalist (d. 1347); Richard
Fitzralph, the opponent of the Mendicant
Orders (Archbishop of Armagh, 1347); and
Thomas Bradwardine, the Doctor Profundus,
the Predestinarian (d. as Archbishop of Canterbury, 1349). Of each of these we may
trace the influence in Wycliffe's writings.
Yet he stands forth as entirely original. In
answer to one who accuses him of taking his
opinions from Ockham, he says : "My convictions owe their origin neither to him nor to me,
but are irrefragably established by Holy Scripture." He was recognised by all his contemporaries at Oxford as the first man among them
in knowledge and in dialectical skill. His
diligence, his resource in argument, his biting
wit, his wealth of illustration, all contributed
to this; but, far more than all, his force of
character and deep conviction, his genuine and
humble piety, and his entire reliance on the

Scriptures. He is never the mere apologist or argumentative fencer, but a preacher of righteousness. In his last complaint to the Parliament (1382) he does not take up a position of self-defence, but boldly demands that, in spite of Pope and bishops, free course should be allowed to the preaching of the true doctrine of the Sacraments.

The time was one of great unsettlement, such as needs a strong man. The English nation was all on fire with the long war with France, at one moment drunk with prosperity, at another dejected by the loss of all its greatness; the Black Death (1348) stalked across Europe and mowed down half the inhabitants of England, producing the usual results of pestilence—panic, recklessness, a dislocation of human relations, and begetting wild hopes by the sudden rise of wages and of prices through the paucity of labourers. The system of the Middle Ages was coming to an end; the Popes had left Rome for Avignon (1305), and their return to Rome in 1376 produced the great schism which shook men's allegiance. Intellectually, also, the world was changing. Scholasticism was waning, the Renaissance

was dawning with Petrarch and Boccaccio.
And there was an uprising of the common
people, not merely to get rid of serfdom, as
under Wat Tyler and John Ball in 1381, but
to gain knowledge, as is witnessed by the poem
of "Piers Plowman," in which Truth reveals
herself, not to the lord or the ecclesiastic, but
to the peasant. Till this time Latin had been
the language of the scholar, the divine, and the
lawyer, as French had been that of the Court;
but now Wycliffe in his Bible and his later
works, Langland in his popular poem, and the
courtly Chaucer in his Tales, laid the founda-
tions of English literature. This in Wycliffe's
case was not so much a literary change as an
appeal to the popular heart, grounded on the
noble belief that simple men are capable of
developing the highest powers : "One simple
man," he says, "if the grace of Christ be in
him, is more profitable to the Church than
many graduates, since he sows Christ's law
humbly and abundantly by work as well as
by word."

The change just noticed, the appeal of the
scholastic divine to the people, is a genuine
product of Christian thought. The Schoolmen

had many authorities to which they appealed
with equal confidence—the Scriptures, the
Fathers, Aristotle, the decrees of Popes and
Councils. Gradually but surely Wycliffe raises
the Scriptures above the rest, and places them
on a pedestal where their unique value is perceived. And, as time goes on, and he is met
by obduracy on the part of those in high place,
he is convinced that it is not learning but
spiritual enlightenment which enables men to
apprehend truth, and he turns to the people ;
the Scriptures must be given to them in their
own tongue, and must be set forth by plain
men in plain words. "If you mix too many
flowers with the seed," he says, "it will not
take root." This led first to the formation of
his own philosophical views on a directly
Scriptural basis, and valuing the simple
teaching of Christ and the Apostles above
all the subtleties of the schools; then to
the translation of the Bible into English,
then to the writing of English sermons and
tracts, and to the training of a body of Poor
Priests, who, like the Franciscans in a former
and the Wesleyans in a later century, went
to and fro among the people, bringing the

simple elements of Divine truth into their
hearts and their homes.

The righteousness of which Wycliffe was the
prophet had to be carried into public life; he
became a legist and a statesman. It is probable
that he sat in Parliament, not only in the
"Good Parliament" of 1376, when the Black
Prince rose from his death-bed to aid the cause
of moral reform in court and council, but also
in 1366, when the question of tribute paid to
the Pope was discussed with great vehemence.
It is known that six Masters of Arts were summoned by the King to that Parliament, and
that Wycliffe speaks of himself as "the King's
own clerk"; that he gives a long account of
the speeches of seven Lords in the debate; and
that he reports certain words of the Bishop of
Rochester as addressed to him "in the public
sitting of Parliament." The tribute of 1,000
marks a year had been imposed on King John
by Innocent III. as the price of the restoration
of the kingdom and the acknowledgment that
the Pope was overlord of England. It had
never been paid willingly, and for thirty-three
years had not been paid at all; the Pope demanded payment with arrears. And this claim

was connected with the numerous exactions of
the Papacy, such as that of the first year's in-
come of all benefices. Arnald, the Pope's
treasurer, had an office in London, at which
these dues or exactions were paid. In the process of the dispute, which lasted many years,
it was shown that the Pope (and a French
Pope living at Avignon) habitually appointed
to English church offices favourites of his own
who never set foot in the realm, and that the
revenues going out of England to the Pope
were four times as large as those paid to the
King. Wycliffe wrote a tract on the oath of
Arnald, taken on his appointment, in which he
swore that he would do nothing contrary to
the interests of the realm, that he would give
good advice to the King, and that he would
conform to the laws of England. In every
particular, as Wycliffe shows, this oath had
been violated; the pecuniary interests of the
Pope had been made to override all law and
justice. The clergy stood by the Pope; but
the laity were grateful to a theologian who
could vindicate the cause of England against
the rapacity of foreigners which was cloaked
with holy sanctions. The Court and the people

stood by him, with hardly an exception, to the end.

It was not as a partisan that Wycliffe took this course, but from a profound sense of justice. Righteousness was more to him than clerical interests. And this led him further. He was sent on an embassy to Bruges in 1374 to treat with the envoys of the Pope on the questions just mentioned ; and at the same time an embassy under John of Gaunt, Duke of Lancaster, was sent to Bruges to make peace with France. Both embassies proved futile ; but the occasion had three important consequences for Wycliffe. First, it made him more fully acquainted with the duplicity of the Pope and of the English clergy who were under his influence ; secondly, it commended him to Lancaster, who ever afterwards stood by him ; and, thirdly, it placed him on an eminence as a patriot when the refusal of the Pope to do justice was debated next year in Parliament.

But Wycliffe was led much further. He saw that the clergy must be brought under the national law. He maintained that the nation had the right, not merely of taxing them (for hitherto they had been exempt), but of depriving them of their estates if this were expedient for the good of the country and of religion. And he came more and more to the conviction that the possession of land, with the feudal position which it implied, was prejudicial to both Church and realm. He even wrote to the Pope exhorting him to disembarrass himself of his temporal sovereignty as an example to the clergy throughout Christendom. The requirements and laws of the country, not the hierarchical position of the clergy, must regulate public policy if righteousness was to prevail.

To these victories he gave systematic expression in his great work "De Dominio." God is the righteous Ruler to whom all sovereignty belongs, but He has given parts of it, as a stewardship, to those who rule under Him, to the Pope and clergy, to the king and magistrates, and to each believer according to his position. Each of these, as holding under Him (for the feudal idea is still dominant), so far as he is faithful to the great Overlord, is supreme in his own sphere. Thus, in contradistinction to the Papal theory (constantly set forth by the image of the plurality of the keys or the two swords in Peter's hands) that the Pope is supreme over all departments of life, Wycliffe asserts the sacredness of the human conscience and human relations in themselves, and their immunity from Papal interference. His more popular tract " On the Six Yokes "—that is, the social relations which are binding on us all— is an anticipation of William Tyndale's " Obedience of a Christian Man." The clergy are to minister faithfully and in subordination to the Scriptures, their faithfulness being judged of by the nation to which they minister; that is their sphere; but in all other spheres the ruler, be he king or father or master, or simple individual, is responsible to God alone. The natural law of human society is the law of God's righteousness.

This sense of the need of righteousness in all departments of life led Wycliffe, in the next place, to recognise the paramount value of the pastoral office above all parts of the Church system. It led him in his old age to leave the University, its philosophy, and its disputations, the scenes of his intellectual triumphs, for a country parish; to esteem the effort to raise

the common life by pastoral intercourse of more
importance than the solitary and unearthly
piety aimed at in monasteries and colleges, and
to bend all his energies to the translation of the
Bible, the issuing of plain English tracts and
sermons, and the training of his Poor Priests.

We may best view the country parson of
those days through the description of him given
by Chaucer, who is supposed to have had
Wycliffe as the model for his picture: "He
was a learned man, a clerk, . . . preaching
Christ's Gospel truly, wonderous diligent,
patient in times of adversity, willing to give
rather than extract from his flock."

Wide was his parish, and houses far asunder,
But he ne left nought ne for rain nor thunder,
In sickness and in mischief to visit
The farthest in his parish, much and lit,
Upon his feet, and in his hand a staff.
This noble example to his sheep he yaf [gave],
That he first wrought, and afterwards he taught.

This description certainly appears to fall in
with the views of the pastoral office which
Wycliffe entertained. The parochial life differs from the monastic in that it brings the
pastor in contact with the common experience

of men and all its varied discipline. It differs also from the life of the evangelist or revival preacher in that it does not touch men merely at one point, but enters into their homes and their business; and it would seem that Wycliffe, like Fitzralph of Armagh, contrasted the life of the parson or " secular " priest with that of the friars on this ground as well as on the ground of their having become corrupt and self-seeking, and of their being the special emissaries of the Pope. It is certain that in his later life he regarded them as a power which did not make for righteousness; so much so that on one occasion, when he was ill, he suddenly roused himself, exclaiming, "I shall not die, but live and declare the works of the Friars." He would have wished the parochial clergy to be married, so that they might be more closely in contact with the life of the people. And we may connect this zeal for parochial well-being with his public spirit and desire for righteousness in the nation; for the parish is a fraction of the nation.

The great instrument for his parochial work and teaching was the English Bible, at which he laboured on, revising and correcting, to the

end of his life. The translation was made
from the Latin Vulgate, for both Greek and
Hebrew were then inaccessible. Wycliffe was
assisted by his friends Nicholas Hereford and
John Purvey, the latter of whom revised the
whole after the Master's death. To this
were added many simple tracts and short
sermons in English (almost all the English
works belong to this time of his life)
which served as guides to his itinerant
preachers.

It would appear that Wycliffe had during
his Oxford days gathered round him a few
scholars whom he trained as preachers. Their
numbers were now largely added to. They
were mostly very simple men, like the first
Franciscans or the first Methodists. Wycliffe
applies to them the word " Idiotes," which was
given to the Apostles by the Sanhedrin. They
went about clad in a long russet gown, preaching and singing in a way which earned them
the name of Lollards (babblers or chaunters),
appealing as men of the people to their own
order, and endeavouring in their rude way
to free religion, especially the sacrament, from
its superstitious elements, and to waken men

up to righteousness and "the law of Christ,"
as Wycliffe constantly called the simple Christianity which he delighted to teach.

But little or nothing would have been done
had Wycliffe's reform not touched the errors of
doctrine which were stifling the Gospel. His
glory is that he attempted to shake the whole
fabric of Papal error. He judged the whole
by its bearing on righteousness. The Pope, so
Wycliffe taught, is to be resisted when acting
unrighteously; the support and allegiance of
the faithful is to be withdrawn from the
clergy when they are untrue to their calling.
The Church is not a body of persons conform-
ing to certain ordinances of which the clergy
hold the key, but the entire body of the elect.
The moral and independent standing which
election implies is all in all. The sacrament
is the receiving of Christ by means of the
sign or emblem; and the change wrought in
the elements is that they become capable of
bringing home the person or presence of Christ
to the believing heart. This, at least, seems to
be the meaning of Wycliffe's expressions, which
are couched in scholastic forms. Transubstan-
tiation, on the other hand, he utterly rejects.

How can the "accidents" of taste or touch remain if the substance is changed? A shrewmouse would detect the fallacy. In the great matter of justification Wycliffe does not take the same ground as Luther; not that he differs from him, but that the aspect of the Gospel which he chiefly realises is not that of conferring the pardon of sin, but that of leading men into living participation in the Divine righteousness. He views the whole process of redemption through the medium of God's sovereignty, and dwells on the election of men to righteousness, though not overriding free will and not admitting the idea of reprobation.

We may see now the way in which Wycliffe was a precursor of the Reformation. He was a prophet nourishing his soul directly from the source of eternal life, not through the media of human inventions, and speaking directly for God and for righteousness. This is indeed the essence of the Reformation doctrine, that we are righteous through faith alone; for what is meant by faith is not some formal belief, or acceptance of some special truth, but the spiritual enlightenment, the expression of the Divine life in the soul, that which "makes evident the things not seen," and "endures as seeing Him who is invisible." This faith Wycliffe possessed in the highest degree. It was this which made him realise the supremacy of Scripture above all writings, and of Christ above all human things, "our only Emperor, Lord, Bishop, and Abbot." It was this which made him assert the Divine sovereignty, with which no human will or invention can conflict. It was this which made him take an independent attitude towards church ordinances, and use them only as conducive to righteousness, but which also gave so high a value in his eyes to plain preaching and the manifestation of truth to the conscience. It was this, finally, which made him assert the independent validity of the gifts or ministries assigned to each believer, and, as a corollary from this, the Divine functions of human government—an assertion which was renewed by the reformers of the sixteenth century only to be buried again beneath a heap of scholastic disputations; an assertion, nevertheless, which needs as much now as in his day to be renewed and made practical if Christianity is ever to master the world.

The meed accorded to Wycliffe was that which the world has usually accorded to the prophets. He was arraigned as a heretic by Courtenay, first as Bishop of London, in 1377, before the Convocation at St. Paul's when he was saved by the appearance at his side of John of Gaunt, who quarrelled violently with the Bishop and prevented any action being taken; and again by the same prelate as Archbishop of Canterbury, at Lambeth, in 1382, when he was saved by the intervention of the Queen Mother, the widow of the Black Prince, and by the threatening attitude of the citizens of London, who honoured him. His University was forced by the Pope and the Archbishop to condemn various propositions from his writings, but he, being present, manfully defended himself; and no one dared either to touch his person or to subject him to excommunication. His advice was sought by the King on his relations with the Pope at the very time when the ecclesiastical power was trying to destroy him; and he continued his work at Lutterworth unimpeded, and, though touched with paralysis in 1383, displayed an astonishing activity in pastoral and literary labours to the end. At length, on the last day of 1384, he was struck down by a second paralytic seizure, during the sacrament, and died with his friends around him.

His body was exhumed in 1428 in pursuance of a decree of the Council of Constance, and his ashes thrown into the Swift. But meanwhile his works had been carried far and wide. In Bohemia, which they reached through those about Anne of Bohemia, wife of Richard II., they inspired new prophets, Hus and Jerome of Prague, who were treacherously put to death for propagating his opinions by the Council of Constance, and gave rise to a national movement which, though quenched in bloodshed, leavened the life of the whole people. In England it was said at the beginning of the fifteenth century that every third man was a Lollard; and the first Parliament of Henry V. was so swayed by Wycliffe's anticlerical principles that the ecclesiastics trembled for their estates. But the renewal of the French wars drew nearly the whole mind of the country in another direction; and the movement of Wycliffe, already compromised during his lifetime by its supposed connection with Wat Tyler's agrarian revolt, was finally discredited when its leader, Sir John Oldcastle, was provoked in 1417 to take arms against his King. But though Lollardry was crushed, the influence of Wycliffe was never extinguished. As many as a hundred and fifty copies of Wycliffe's Bible still remain ; and there is no doubt that it was widely read by the common people, for whom it was written, throughout the fifteenth century. When, in 1510, a raid against heretics was made by Fitzjames, Bishop of London, so violent that Colet wrote to Erasmus that all the prisons were full of them, the articles in almost all cases stated that the accused possessed copies of Wycliffe's Bible or of some of his works; and Erasmus, in his account of his pilgrimage to the shrine of Becket, at Canterbury, when he tells how his companion (Colet) questioned the advantage of such an exhibition of relics, represents his interlocutor as saying : " Who was your friend ? Some Wycliffite, I suppose." Thus the reformer of the four-

teenth century joins hands with the reformer
of the sixteenth.

And thus it is ever with the prophet.   " In
the sight of the unwise he seems to die," but
" his hope is full of immortality "; his spirit
lives on and prepares men for the better day.

VII.

MARTIN LUTHER, THE PROPHET OF THE REFORMATION.

By Professor
ADOLF HARNACK.

MARTIN LUTHER, THE PROPHET OF THE REFORMATION.

He came in the fulness of time—when the rule of the Roman Church, which had hitherto educated the peoples, had become a tyranny, when States and nations were beginning to throw off an ecclesiastical yoke and independently to organise themselves in accordance with their own laws.

He came in the fulness of time—when the economic conditions of Europe, both through inner developments and through the discovery of distant lands, had become completely changed, and the method of administration of their estates by the Roman priests and monks was no longer tenable.

He came in the fulness of time—when mediæval churchly science had outlived its usefulness, and when the tree of knowledge was producing young, fresh shoots.

He came in the fulness of time — when the classes and casts of the Middle Ages were disintegrating, and when everywhere the individual, supported by the new culture of the Renaissance, was striving to struggle up to independence. He came when the monastic idea of life had run through all phases of its development, and when man was beginning to esteem an active not less than an ascetic life.

He came in the fulness of time—when laymen were no longer satisfied with priest and sacrament, but were seeking God Himself, and were feeling the personal responsibility of their own souls. He came as man was recognising the precepts of the Church to be but arbitrary laws, and her traditions as only innovations and forgeries.

He was no universal genius, no Plato, no Leibnitz. He did not grasp all the conditions of his time ; nay, he did not even know them all. His education was mediocre. He was no sharp and refined thinker, he was no humanist, he was no critic ; his vocation was not to rectify theoretical errors just before they were errors. The sphere of science was not his sphere ;

indeed, he had an instinctive and never entirely conquered suspicion of "reason."

He was no saint, no Francis, who, through the glow of feeling, through the sweetness of his spirit or the power of his sacrifice, swept every one along with him. He was also no agitator, no orator, who, like Savonarola, could move and inflame the masses.

Luther was no cosmopolitan, but a German with the marked characteristics of his nation, a German as monk, as professor, and as reformer. His personality has never been understood by the Romanic races; it has never impressed them; his thoughts alone have been able to take root among them.

How was this man, then, able to become the reformer of the Western Church? How was it that this professor in a little German university, in the midst of an uncultivated environment, could unfetter the great movement by which the new epoch in the history of the world began? How did it happen that, through him, "the time was fulfilled"? He was in only one thing great and mighty, over-whelmingly and irresistibly the master of his time, victoriously overcoming the history of a

8

thousand years in order to force his age into new channels. *He was great only in the redis-covered knowledge of God in the Gospels.* What it means to have a God, what this God is, how He grasps us, and how we can apprehend and hold Him—all that he experienced and that he proclaimed. In the midst of the night of his conventual life, as he strove to work out his salvation in fear and trembling, it dawned upon him like the sun: "The just shall live *by faith.*" In the midst of the complex system of what was called "religion," in the midst of unsatisfying consolations and of incomplete penances, he lived *religion itself,* and he led it out into freedom. The living God—not a philosophical or mystic abstraction—the mani-fest and gracious God, was a God to be reached by every Christian. Unchangeable reliance of the heart upon God, personal confidence of belief in Him who said, "I am thy salvation," that was to Luther the whole sum of religion. Beyond all care and trouble, beyond all arts of the ascetic, beyond all theological precepts, he dared to grasp God Himself, and in this deed of faith his whole life won its independent sturdi-ness. " Mit unser Macht ist Nichts gethan "

("With our might is nothing done"). He
knew the might which gives to our lives both
firmness and freedom; he knew that might, and
he called it by its name, Belief. To him that
meant no longer an obedient acceptance of
ecclesiastical dogmas, it meant no knowledge, no
deed, but simply the personal and continual
giving of the heart to God, a daily regeneration
of man. That was his confession of faith, a
living, busy, active thing, a sure trust, making
one joyful and eager in the sight of God and
man, something which makes us always ready
to serve or to suffer. Despite all evil, yes,
despite our sin and guilt, our life is hid in God,
when we trust Him as children trust their
father. That was the vital thought and the
vital power of Luther's life.

With equal certainty he perceived and
experienced the other idea, the idea of "the
freedom of a Christian." This freedom was to
him no empty emancipation or the licence for
every whim. Freedom meant to Luther the
liberation from every external or human
authority in matters of belief and conscience.
Christian freedom was to him the feeling of
surety that, united with God, he was raised

above the world, sin, death, and the devil. "If
God be for us, who can be against us?" Every
soul that has found God, and in Him has
recognised its refuge, is free—so proclaimed
Luther.

> Ein' feste Burg ist unser Gott,
> Ein' gute Wehr und waffen.

> (A mighty fortress is our God,
> A bulwark never failing.)

Let it be here remarked that, in the same
hymn, Luther asks:

> Fragst du, wer er ist?
> Er heisset Jesus Christ,
> Der Herr Zebaoth,
> Und ist kein and'rer Gott.

> (Dost ask who that may be?
> Christ Jesus, it is he,
> His name, Lord Sabaoth;
> Nor is there other God.)

In Jesus Christ alone Luther recognised
God. Outside of Christ he saw only a dark,
frightful, and enigmatical Force. In Christ
alone he saw the gracious God. Luther was
no philosopher who would recognise God in the
construction of the world; he was no mystic,

who could raise God out of his own soul's secret depths. He was a faithful son of the Christian Church, convinced that she was in the right with her commission from Jesus Christ. He was a faithful disciple of Paul, and had learned from him that all knowledge of God lies locked up in the sentence, " God is the Father of our Lord Jesus Christ." He was a faithful disciple of Christ Himself, who said " No man knoweth the Father save only the Son, and him to whom the Son will reveal Him."

Not only did Luther win God-knowledge in Jesus Christ, "the mirror of God's paternal heart," but also the fact that Jesus is the Redeemer, who through death has freed us from sin and blame. Paul's Gospel is also Luther's. Before the latter, no one in the Church really understood the Epistles to the Romans and to the Galatians. Just because he was convinced that he was putting the old, dimmed Gospel again in the light, he was far from the thought of adding anything to it. Never had he another plan than that *of restoring the old belief;* never did he think to fight against the Church, but always *for the Church*

against a false and soul-dangerous practice;
never did he dream that the Gospel had been
really lost—no, but it was to be freed from a
captivity into which the Pope, the priests, and
the theologians had led it.

Great, lasting reformations are made only by
conservative men; not those who "destroy,"
but those who "fulfil," bring about a new era.
Luther—at the bottom of his heart the most
conservative of men—has broken the mediæval Catholic system in pieces for millions of
souls, and thus freed the history of progressive
humanity from the shackles of that system.
In that he vindicated the new and yet old
Gospel, in that he freed the conscience of the
individual from priest and statute, he struck
deadly blows against the Church of the Middle
Ages. For (1) he overturned her teaching as
to salvation—salvation not being a thing
brought about by donations and merits, but
the free grace of God, which gives us the conviction that we are His children. (2) He overturned the teaching as to Christian perfection
—true Christian life does not consist in mo-
nasticism, but in an active life of fidelity to a
calling, in humility, patience, and the service

of love to our neighbour.   (3) He overturned
the teachings as regards the sacrament—God
does not give us individual and different frag-
ments of grace, but He gives us the forgiveness
of sins and with it all grace, yes, He gives us
Himself as the Bread of our lives.   (4) He
overturned the priestly Church-system—God
wills that all His children shall be priests, and
He has instituted but one office, the office of
proclaiming the Gospel and of distributing forgiveness.   (5) Luther overturned the mediæval
church services—God will not be honoured
by means of ceremonies, masses, oblations, &c.,
but only through praise and thanksgiving,
pleading and prayer.   Every church service
must be spiritual, and at the same time innately
bound with service to one's neighbour.   (6) He
overturned the false authorities of Roman
Catholicism.   Not the Pope, nor the Councils,
not even the letter of the Bible (yet here, in
regard to the Bible, Luther was himself not
completely clear), has unerring authority, but
only the Gospel, the power and truth of which
the soul inwardly knows.

All these points have to do with religion
alone.   Luther determined to purify religion

and to free it from every strange thing which does not belong to it. Besides this he never had another independent interest; he did not care about bettering the world, or the State, or science, for themselves alone. Yet right here is revealed the truth of the saying: "Seek ye first the kingdom of God and His righteousness, and all these things shall be added unto you." In that Luther thought out the Gospel in all its parts, proclaimed and applied it, all else fell into his lap; in that he liberated religion from mixture with that which is foreign to it, *he also liberated the natural life and the natural order of things.* He put everything in its right place, and gave everything freedom and room for development. Everywhere he broke apart unnatural ties, he loosed old chains, he gave air and light.

Theology through him is henceforth to be nothing else than the exposition of the Gospel, of how it has founded the Christian community and still keeps it together. The proof of theology is no longer derived from external authority or strange philosophical speculations, but by the simple fact of Christ's appearance, and by our inward experience.

Philosophy is no longer a feared servant or a seductive mistress of theology, but her independent sister. Languages and history are studied conscientiously and faithfully, in order to ascertain the right meaning of every word.

The State is no longer regarded as a half-sinful product of compulsion and need, and the creature of the Church, but as the God-willed, independent order of public social life.

Law does not longer pass as a dangerous middle course, something between the might of the stronger and the virtue of the Christian, but as the independent, God-given rule of intercourse always maintained by the "powers that be."

Marriage is no longer thought of as a Divine concession towards the weak, but as a free bond between the sexes, a bond instituted by God, and free from tutelage on the part of the Church, and as the school of the highest morality.

General benefactions, such as the care of the poor, are not now so much pursued because of any desire to assure one's own salvation; they have become a free service to one's neighbour, the final scope and only reward of which is effective relief.

Above all things, however, in civil (as opposed to ecclesiastical) callings, activity in house and farm, in trade and official position, is no longer looked upon suspiciously as if it led away from our spiritual vocation. Men now know that the one who guides a household well, educates children patiently and faithfully, fulfils the duties of a calling—even though that one be but a poor boy or a lowly maid—stands in the rightful spiritual place and is higher than all monks and nuns.

Over the great period which we call the Middle Ages, over the chaos of non-independent and intricate forms, there soared the spirit of belief, which had recognised its own nature and therefore had also recognised its limits. Under its sway, all things that had a right to free existence now strove towards independent development. Before Luther, no one had ever separated so clearly and distinguishingly the great departments of life, and given to each its own right. Wonderful! this man would not teach the world other than what the being, the power, and the comfort of the Christian religion is ; but in that he recognised this most important department in its own individuality, all other departments came to their own. Luther preached that the just man lives by faith, and that a child of God is a free master over all things. In that he so taught he indeed freed men and things, and thus showed that "the time was fulfilled," for he was called that the time should be fulfilled.

He became *the* reformer. Beside him Zwingli and Calvin can claim but second places; they are dependent on him. Yes, we can even say : *He was the Reformation.* He had experienced the Reformation in his own soul, when he struggled in the cloister with the creed of his Church. Everything which he afterwards said, wrote, and did, in Wittenberg, in Worms, and in Coburg, was only the natural consequence of that experience. Out of his breast, from the bottom of his heart, the Reformation streamed as a brook out of hidden springs in the rock. In one sense he did not give power and endurance to the Reformation : he did not set its bounds and aim, but the Reformation gushed from his spirit like a fruitful stream. "Here I stand ; I can do no other," said he, before

Emperor and Empire. When the lonely man thus spoke, it was decided that he, through his faith, like Abraham, should become the father of many thousands; it was decided that a great epoch in the history of mankind had finished its course, and a new was advancing.

But we must not forget that it was four hundred years ago that Luther taught. The convenient belief that he thought out everything for us, and that we can rest on his teaching, is a foolish one. The greatest hero is always only a *finisher* for the past; as regards the future he is but a *beginner*. He who does not understand Luther so that he learns from him the spirit with which to solve new problems and lessons, and so that he endeavours to continue the Reformer's work, understands him falsely. The prophets have been given to us, not that we should build their graves, but that we should inflame our hearts through their faith and their courage.

VIII.

JOHN WESLEY.

By the Very Rev.
F. W. FARRAR, D.D.

VIII.

JOHN WESLEY.

It has often happened that the most memorable revolutions or reawakenments in the moral and spiritual world have been achieved by men who were not remarkable either for learning or for genius. St. Francis of Assisi awoke the Church of the thirteenth century from its gorgeous dreams of dominion and luxury, and has eternised his name on the bright lists of sainthood ; but the humble brown figure of the poor illiterate wanderer looks absolutely insignificant beside the purpureal stateliness of Pope Innocent III. There was something almost bourgeois in the plain homeliness of St. Vincent de Paul, yet in founding his sisterhoods of mercy he inaugurated the chief movements of social philanthropy. Thomas Clarkson and John Howard were simple country squires, with no remarkable endowments of any kind except the genius of goodness and

the sensibility of compassion, yet the one ended
the slave trade and emancipated the slave,
and the other—traversing Europe, as Edmund
Burke said, "to dive into the depths of dun-
geons, to plunge into the infection of hospitals,
to take the gauge and dimensions of misery, de-
pression, and contempt "—purified the prisons
of the Christian world from their enormous
abuses and dehumanised loathliness.   There
were many noblemen of the last generation
who towered over the late Earl of Shaftesbury in the splendour of their attainments and
their oratory, yet none of them, not one of
the Archbishops, Bishops, and great ecclesiastics of his day, effected one tithe of his mighty
work of beneficence for the poor women of the
mines and collieries, for the factory children,
for the little "climbing boys," for the waifs
and strays and gutter-children of London, for
the costermongers, for maltreated lunatics, and
for hosts of the oppressed.   To this order of
men, though he was superior to them in learning, belonged John Wesley.   He found a Church
forgetful and neglectful of its duties, somnolent
in the plethora of riches, and either unmindful
or unwisely mindful of the poor.   He found

churches empty, dirty, neglected, crumbling into hideous disrepair; he found the work of the ministry performed in a manner scandalously perfunctory; he found in the ranks of the priesthood more than enow

> of such as, for their bellies' sake,
> Creep, and intrude, and climb into the fold.
>
> *   *   *   *   *
>
> And, when they list, their lean and flashy songs
> Grate on their scrannel pipes of wretched straw;
> The hungry sheep look up, and are not fed,
> But, swoln with wind and the rank mist they
>   draw,
> Rot inwardly, and foul contagion spread;
> Besides what the grim wolf, with privy paw,
> Daily devours apace, and nothing said,

Doubtless in his day, as in Milton's, it might have been said,

> But that two-handed engine at the door
> Stands ready to smite once, and smite no more.

But John Wesley, becoming magnetic with moral sincerity, flashed into myriads of hearts fat as brawn, cold as ice, hard as the nether millstone, the burning spark of his own intense convictions, and thus he saved the Church, which at first had nothing for him but sneers, hatred, and persecution. Wesley never was an

enemy to the Church of England. He loved
the Church which hated him. He included her
name in his daily "grace before meat." He
died in her full communion. He would have
said, as sincerely as Edmund Burke, "I wish to
see the Church of England great and powerful;
I wish to see her foundation laid low and deep;
I would have her open wide her hospitable
gates by a liberal comprehension; I would
have her a common blessing to the world, an
example, if not an instructor, to those who
have not the happiness to belong to her; I
would have her give a lesson of peace to mankind, that a vexed and wandering generation
may be taught to seek refuge and toleration in
the bosom of her maternal charity." And he
distinctly saved the Church of England from
the Nemesis of just retribution, which but for
him would sooner or later have overwhelmed
her in indiscriminate collapse, and might not
improbably have buried under her heaps of
ruin all that was best in the great heritage of
English religion. He set her the example
of indefatigable activity, of immense and un-
grudging self-sacrifice, of that true beauty of
holiness which shines in the life of every Chris-

tian who "makes his moral being his prime
care," and gives the actual, not the merely
nominal, sovereignty to the beliefs which he
professes to regard as supreme. He saved the
Church of England, though at first she so an-
grily and contemptuously rejected him, and,
just as from the mouth of Socrates issued forth

> Mellifluous streams which watered all the schools
> Of Academics old and new, with those
> Surnamed Peripatetics, and the sect
> Epicurean, and the Stoic severe,

so, from the impulse which Wesley gave, origi-
nated almost every form of special religious
enthusiasm since his day. Thus he became one
of the most disinterested of those benefactors
of mankind who "have raised strong arms to
bring heaven a little nearer to our earth."

One great virtue in his character was that
sovereign religious tolerance which is so infinitely rare amid the divergences of religious
shibboleths. In the first century the heathen
said, "See how these Christians love one another"; but, long before the third century, the
odium theologicum had culminated in those execrable forms of religious virulence which, if
"love" be indeed the fulfilling of the law, are

the very antithesis of the Christlike spirit, at
which all *profess* to aim who take Christ for an
ensample that they should walk in His steps.
It is a splendid testimony to Wesley's moral
insight and spiritual greatness that " no reformer the world has ever seen so united faithfulness to the essential doctrines of Revelation
with charity towards men of every Church and
creed." This spirit of John Wesley has been
found, theoretically at least, only in the best
and greatest Christians.

Bishop Sanderson pointed out to some of the
narrowest of the post-Reformation sectaries that
" the Church was not to be confined to the narrow pingle of a room in Amsterdam." William
Penn uttered the great sentiment, so dear to
the heart of Abraham Lincoln, that the meek,
the just, the pious, the devout, are everywhere
of one religion, and that when death hath taken
off these masks they will know and love one another. The devout Dominican Henri Feyrrane
saw, as Lacordaire also saw, that the worst possible policy is " to make the gate of the Church
bristle with anathemas, as with razors and
pitchforks." But too many nominal Christians have forgotten that all these words and

actions tend to reduce the Church to the same
deplorable chaos of mutual hatreds and fierce
disdain which Christ found among the Pharisees and Sadducees of Jerusalem, when He
chose the hated and heretical Samaritan as
His exemplary type of the goodness which loved
its neighbour.

I dwell on this high virtue of Wesley because
it is so exceptional, and because it was never
more needed than in these days. Writing
in advanced age to the Bishop of Lincoln, he
said: "Alas! my Lord, is this a time to per-
secute any man for conscience' sake? I be-
seech you do as you would be done to. You
are a man of sense; you are a man of learning;
nay, I verily believe (what is of infinitely more
value) you are a man of piety. Then think
and let think." Again, how wise are the remarks in the preface to his Sermons: "Some
may say I have mistaken the way myself, though
I have undertaken to teach others. It is very
possible that I have. But I trust, whereinso-
ever I have been mistaken, my mind is open to
conviction. I sincerely desire to be better in-
formed. What I know not, teach thou me.
'Da mihi scire,' as says St. Augustine, 'quod

sciendum est.'   If I linger in the path I have
been accustomed to tread, . . . take me by
the hand and lead me. . . . But be not dis-
couraged if I ask you not to beat me down in
order to quicken my pace.   May I request you
further not to give me hard names in order to
bring me into the right way? . . . For
God's sake, if it be possible, let us not provoke
one another to wrath.   Let us not kindle in each
other this fire of hell.   If we could discern
truth by that dreadful light, would it not be
loss rather than gain?   For how far is love,
even with many wrong opinions, to be preferred
before truth itself without love!   We may die
without the knowledge of many truths, and yet
be carried into Abraham's bosom.   But if we
die without love, what will knowledge avail?
Just as much as it avails the devil and his
angels! "

The ground for this wise and noble tolerance,
which is one of Wesley's special lessons to this
religiously distracted age, was his clear realisa-
tion of the truth—demonstrated by all history
—that while unity of spirit is attainable, uni-
formity of organisation is not; that while there
can be but one flock of the Good Shepherd,

there always have been and to the end of time there will be many folds. Dean Stanley delighted in a story—I know not its source and will not vouch for its authenticity—which he called "Wesley's Dream." It told how Wesley dreamt that, wandering to the gate of Gehenna, he asked whether there were any Romanists, any Anglicans, any Baptists, any Calvinists, any Independents there, and was told in each case, "Yes, a great many," and was yet more deeply pained when, asking, "And are there any Wesleyans here?" it was still answered, "Yes, a great many." Then, returning to the gate of Heaven, he asked, "Are there any Romanists here?" "None whatever." "Any Anglicans?" "None whatever." "Any Baptists?" "None whatever. "Any Calvinists?" "None whatever." "Any Wesleyans?" Still none whatever. "Whom then have you here?" he asked in amazement. "We have none but Christians here," was the answer; "we know no other name." Whether the story was a pleasing allegory of the Dean's or not I cannot tell; but this I know, that Wesley's sermon on the Catholic Spirit would have the honour of being thought shockingly

lax by bigots of every denomination, yet all
true Christians might well say with him, "I
desire to have a league, offensive and defensive,
with every soldier of Christ. We have all not
only one Lord, one faith, one baptism, but we
are all also engaged in one warfare."

As another of Wesley's exemplary qualities
I would single out his sovereign common
sense, which is also an endowment much liable
to overthrow by the violences of egotistical
dogmatism. Though many have identified his
teaching mainly with certain formulæ, Wesley
had no faith in the bare reiteration of shibboleths. His idea of a "Gospel sermon" was
not the narrowly ignorant one, which supposes
it to consist in the incessant repetition of
phrases—phrases often originally meaningless
to many of those who used them, or which have
become stereotyped into mere inanity and fetich-
ism. In his diary for November 20, 1785, he
writes: "I preached in Bethnal Green, and
spoke as plainly as I possibly could, on having
a form of godliness but denying the power
thereof. And this I judged far more suitable
to such a congregation than talking about justification by faith." How free, again, from all

hysteric excitability was the entire attitude of
his religion ! Some one had been talking in an
exaggerated and fantastic way about death, and
asking what he would do if he knew that he
would die the next day. "What should I do?"
he said. "Exactly what I shall do now. I
should call and talk to Mr. So-and-so and Mrs.
So-and-so ; and dine at such an hour, and preach
in the evening, and have supper, and then I
should go to bed and sleep as soundly as ever I
did in my life." His feeling about death was
that, so far from being terrible, it was man's
great birthright; and he would say, with the
poet :

To you the thought of death is terrible,
Having such hold on life; to me it is not :
No more than is the lifting of a latch,
Or as a step into the open air
Out of a tent already luminous
With light that shines through its transparent folds.

Again, it was no small matter that, in an age so
corrupt and decadent as his, in which the
dregs of sensuality and worldliness poured
over the glorious England of Puritanism by
the despicable epoch of the Restoration had
reduced religion to a Dead Sea of torpid

unreality, Wesley, like the great Hebrew prophets of old, should have stood forth as a preacher of righteousness. No preacher or reformer can effect great results unless he insists upon Christ's plain teaching that, if we would ever enter into the kingdom of heaven, we must keep the commandments. Late in his career he said: "Near fifty years ago a great and good man, Dr. Potter, then Archbishop of Canterbury, gave me an advice for which I have ever since had occasion to bless God. 'If you desire to be extensively useful, do not spend your time and strength in contending for or against such things as are of a disputable nature, but in testifying against open and notorious vice and in prompting real spiritual holiness.' Let us keep to this, leaving a thousand disputable points to those that have no better business than to toss the ball of controversy to and fro, and let us bear a faithful testimony in our several stations against all ungodliness and unrighteousness, and with all our might recommend that inward and outward holiness without which no man shall see the Lord."

It may be, as I have said, that in talent, in

imagination, in learning, in the pure and un-
definable quality of genius, Wesley was not the
equal of many of his contemporaries; but
which among them all equalled him in versa-
tility of beneficence, in zeal of self-sacrifice, in
the munificence of his generosity, or in the
lustre of the example which he has left to all
the world? Consider his supreme disinterested-
ness, his unparalleled courage, his indefatigable
toils. How many have there been in all the
centuries who made such an absolute offering
of his money to God, and, living on less than
many a curate's salary, gave away £40,000?
Consider, again, his unparalleled courage.
How many have shown equal undauntedness?
Men admire the courage of the soldier who
heads the forlorn hope through the cross-fire
of the batteries, of the sailor or of the fireman,
who, at personal risk, plucks from destruction
an imperilled life; but such physical courage is
a million times cheaper and more common than
that of the scholar, the gentleman, the clergyman, who in that age, day after day, month after
month, year after year, in England, in America,
in Scotland, in Wales, in Ireland, even in the
Isle of Man, could, voluntarily and out of the

pure love of souls, face raging mobs and descend
to what was then regarded as the vulgar humiliation of preaching in the open air. And higher
even than this was the moral and spiritual
courage which, in the calm of blameless inno-
cence, could treat the most atrocious and the
most persistent calumnies with the disdainful
indifference of unblemished rectitude. When
even Charles Wesley was thrown into a fever
of agonised excitement by the scandal against
his brother caused by his wife's publication
of stolen, forged, or interpolated letters, and
wanted him to stay in London and expose the
slander, John Wesley remained perfectly calm,
knowing that no real harm can befall

> The virtuous mind that ever walks attended
> By a strong-siding champion Conscience.

"Brother," he said, "when I devoted to God
my ease, my time, my life, did I exempt my
reputation?" Then consider his indefatigable
toils—those sixty-eight years of service; the
4,400 miles which he travelled yearly on the
execrable roads of those days; the 225,000
miles which he traversed in his lifetime; the
42,400 sermons—sometimes as many as fifteen

a week—which he preached even after his return from Georgia—preached mostly in the
open air, and sometimes to as many as 20,000
souls; those endless meetings, those burden-
some anxieties, those numerous publications,
that love of so many communities, continued
amid incessant attacks of the mob, the pulpit,
and the press, and scarcely ever relaxed till
the patriarchal age of eighty-eight. Could a
clergyman of any denomination, amid the work
which, in comparison to his toils, is but ease
and supineness, think it anything but an
honour to profess reverence for the memory
of one who so heroically lived and so nobly
died? Although the world and the Church
have learned to be comparatively generous to
Wesley now that a hundred years have sped
away, and though the roar of contemporary
scandal has long since ceased, I doubt whether
even now he is at all adequately appreciated.
I doubt whether many are aware of the extent
to which to this day the impulse to every great
work of philanthropy and social reformation
has been due to his energy and insight. The
British and Foreign Bible Society, the Religious Tract Society, the London Missionary

Society, even the Church Missionary Society,
owe not a little to his initiative. The vast
spread of religious instruction by weekly peri-
odicals, and the cheap press with all its stu-
pendous consequences, were inaugurated by
him. He gave a great extension to Sunday-
schools and the work of Robert Raikes. He
gave a great impulse both to national education and to technical education, and in starting
the work of Silas Told, the Foundry Teacher,
he anticipated the humble and holy work of
John Pounds, the Portsmouth cobbler. He
started in his own person the funeral reform,
which is only now beginning to attract public
attention, when in his will he directed that
at his obsequies there should be no hearse, no
escutcheon, no coach, no pomp. He visited
prisons and ameliorated the lot of prisoners
before John Howard ; and his very last letter
was written to stimulate William Wilberforce
in his Parliamentary labours for the emancipation of the slave. When we add to this the
revival of fervent worship and devout hymno-
logy among Christian congregations, and their
deliverance from the drawling doggerel of
Sternhold and Hopkins, and the frigid nullities

of Tate and Brady, we have indeed shown how
splendid was the list of his achievements, and
that, as Isaac Taylor says, he furnished " the
starting-point for our modern religious history
in all that is characteristic of the present time."

And yet, even in this long and splendid cata-
logue, we have not mentioned his greatest and
most distinctive work, which was that through
him to the poor the Gospel was preached. Let
Whitefield have the credit of having been the
first to make the green grass his pulpit and the
heaven his sounding-board; but Wesley in-
stantly followed, at all costs, the then daring
example, and, through all evil report and all
furious opposition, he continued it until at
last at Kingswood, at the age of eighty-one,
he preached in the open-air, under the shade
of trees which he himself had planted, and sur-
rounded by the children and children's children
of his own disciples, who had long since passed
away. Overwhelming evidence exists to show
what preaching was before and in his day;
overwhelming evidence exists to show what
the Church and people of England were before
and in his day—how dull, how vapid, how
soulless, how Christless was the preaching;

how torpid, how Laodicean was the Church ;
how godless, how steeped in immorality
was the land. To Wesley was mainly granted
the task, for which he was set apart by the
hands of invisible consecration, the task which
even an archangel might have envied him,
of awakening a mighty revival of religious
life in those dead pulpits, in that slumbering
Church, in that corrupt society. His was the
religious sincerity which not only founded the
Wesleyan community, but, working through
the heart of the very Church which had
despised him, flashed fire into her whitening
embers. Changing its outward forms, the
work of John Wesley caused first the Evangelical movement, then the High Church
movement ; and in its enthusiasm of humanity,
has even reappeared in all that is best in the
humble Salvationists, who learned from the
example of Wesley what Bishop Lightfoot
called "that lost secret of Christianity, the
compulsion of human souls." Recognising no
utterance of authority as equally supreme with
that which came to him from the Sinai of
conscience, Wesley did the thing and scorned
the consequence. His was the voice which

offered hope to the despairing and welcome to
the outcast. His was the voice which, sound-
ing forth over the Valley of Dry Bones, cried,
"Come from the four winds, O breath, and
breathe upon these slain that they may live."
The poet says:

> Of those three hundred grant but three
> To make a new Thermopylæ.

And when I think of John Wesley, the organ-
iser, of Charles Wesley, the poet, of George
Whitefield, the orator of this mighty movement, I feel inclined to say of those three self-
sacrificing and holy men, Grant but even one
to help in the mighty work which yet remains
to be accomplished! Had we but three such
now,

> Hoary-headed selfishness would feel
> His death-blow, and would totter to his grave;
> A brighter light attend the human day,
> When every transfer of earth's natural gift
> Should be a commerce of good words and works.

We have, it is true, hundreds of faithful
workers in the Church of England and in
other religious communities. But for the
slaying of dragons, the rekindlement of

10

irresistible enthusiasm, the redress of intolerable wrongs, a Church needs many Pentecosts
and many Resurrections. And these, in the
providence of God, are brought about, not
by committees and conferences and common
workers, but by men who escape the average;
by men who come forth from the multitude;
by men who, not content to trudge on in the
beaten paths of commonplace and the cart-ruts
of routine, go forth, according to their Lord's
command, into the highways and hedges; by
men in whom the love of God burns like a
consuming flame upon the altar of the heart;
by men who have become electric to make
myriads of other souls thrill with their own
holy zeal. Such men are necessarily rare, but
God's richest boon to any nation, to any
society, to any church, is the presence and
work of such a man—and such a man was John
Wesley.

The bust placed in Westminster Abbey to
the memory of John Wesley, more than twenty
years ago, was a very tardy recognition of the
vast debt of gratitude which England owes to
him. It stands hard by the cenotaph of that
other illustrious Nonconformist, Isaac Watts,

and gives the beautiful presentment of the aged
face of the evangelist and the fine features
of Charles, his poet-brother. In the solemn
aisle thousands of visitors to our great Temple
of Silence and Reconciliation may read three of
his great sayings—one, so full of holy energy,
"I look on all the world as my parish";
another, so full of bright and holy confidence,
" God buries His workmen, but continues His
work "; the third, when, on his deathbed,
uplifting victoriously his feeble and emaciated
arm, he said: "The best of all is, God is with
us." "Yes ! " he exclaimed again, in a tone
of victorious rapture, "the best of all is, God
is with us."

IX.

JONATHAN EDWARDS.

By the Rev.

A. M. FAIRBAIRN, D.D.

IX.

JONATHAN EDWARDS.

Jonathan Edwards is a thinker difficult to appreciate and very easy to misunderstand. His faults lie on the surface, while his merits are to be discovered only by sympathetic study. He is not only the greatest of all the thinkers that America has produced, but also the highest speculative genius of the eighteenth century. What in him was occasional most impressed his own generation and most easily arrests the eye of ours. What in him was permanent retreats from the hands that hastily glean in the field of literature and religion. What most impresses a cocksure and sceptical critic like Mr. Leslie Stephen is the awfulness of Edwards's descriptions of sin and its punishment; and he marvels that any writer could say anything concerning him without dwelling on his doctrine of hell. But the grim and terrible sermons which Mr. Stephen quotes as if they were the

essence of Edwards's mind were not the crea-
tions of his reason, which was Edwards's master
faculty, but the work of his imagination, hand-
ling in a super-sensitive mood material it had
inherited—*i.e.*, they were epic pictures thrown
out while his imagination was intoxicated with
spiritual passion or as it were drenched by
the wave of religious enthusiasm then rolling
over New England. In truth, the distinctive
theology of Edwards was of quite another
order, the creation of a reason all alive
with speculative passion, and moved as if
by an infinite hunger for the Divine. In him
religious affection was exalted and transfigured
by an illuminative yet inexorable reason, a
thought that, urged by the necessity of its own
being, could know no rest till it had, not simply
grasped the skirts, but, as it were, penetrated
to the very heart of Deity. In a far higher
degree than Spinoza he was a " God-intoxicated
man," and his religious affection more than
Spinoza's intellectual love made man one in
will through being one in heart with God.
The development from Edwards emphasized
too much what was occasional, while it emphasized too little what was permanent ; and so

the New England becomes more a scholastic than a speculative theology, while, if it had been true to the genius and soul of Edwards, it would have been more speculative and less scholastic.

In the attempt to understand him we have first to realise the comparative isolation in which he lived, and therefore the independence with which he worked. If we put him back into his time without recollection of his place, no man could seem less the son of his century. He was born in 1703, the year before Locke died. In England Deism had commenced its belligerent and barren career. Berkeley had entered Trinity College, and was jotting down in his commonplace book the speculations that were later to become a new "Theory of Vision," and furnish the "Principles of Human Knowledge." Toland was busy proving Christianity not mysterious, and arguing for a new Theism which should make God all in all. Of those who may be regarded as more strictly his contemporaries, Joseph Butler entered Oriel College, Oxford, just about the time Edwards entered Yale. David Hume, eight years his junior, became, like Edwards, a student of Locke, but, unlike him, so interpreted Locke

as to deduce from him a system of universal
doubt, which did not, like that of Descartes,
spare thought and find through the ego a way
into reasoned belief. In France, in the very
year of Edwards's birth, Voltaire entered, a boy
of nine, the great Jesuit School, the College
Louis le Grand, and began to prepare himself
to conduct his crusade—in its essence more
Christian than those of the Middle Ages—
against the tyranny of the unreal and make-
believe in religion. While Edwards was pastor in Northampton Rousseau was indulging
himself in all the luxury of sentiment, and
feeling his way towards the limitation of the
individual and the construction of society
through the Social Contract.   As Edwards,
diffident in secular things while greatly daring
in intellectual, was describing to the corpora-
tion of Princeton his " peculiarly unhappy constitution, attended with flaccid solids, vapid,
sizy, and scarce fluids, and a low tide of
spirits ; often occasioning a kind of childish
weakness and contemptibleness of speech, presence, and demeanour, with a disagreeable dul-
ness and stiffness, much unfitting me for
conversation, but more especially for the gov-

ernment of a college," and so hesitating to accept the position offered to him—a younger contemporary in Germany, Lessing, was turning his thoughts to the reform of the theatre, and to a more scientific interpretation of religion and its history.

But Edwards in his New England home lived apart from all these European movements and influences. They could, indeed, hardly be said to have touched him. As a student he had studied the "Essay on the Human Understanding," and through it discovered at once his faculty and his problem. In Dr. Samuel Johnson of Stratford, and in Cutler, his tutor, he had met men who knew something of Berkeley; the former, in particular, being a convinced idealist. And, indeed, while Edwards was beginning his career as a pastor, Berkeley was attempting to make a home for himself in Rhode Island. But while there are points where he coincides with Berkeley, Edwards's development was independent; they agree rather by logical coincidence than by literary or speculative imitation. And this is the more significant as the agreements are mainly on points which Berkeley later developed, and where he agreed with

Malebranche.   Edwards, indeed, largely worked
out his problems, not only in independence, but
in an intellectual isolation which no man in the
Old World could know; least of all was it
known to the men with whom he has most
affinity—Spinoza, Malebranche, and Berkeley.
The shape which both the problems and their
solution assumed at his subtle hands proceeded
as much from his simple and pure nature as
from the simplicity of the life he lived. The
faith of his people possessed him. Time was
to him eternal; every year, every day, and
every hour were the dwelling-place of God.
The God he believed in moved all things, filled
all time and every place. Yet his individual
existence was not a mere moment in the being
of the Eternal, but a means by which God real-
ised His purposes in time and fulfilled His ends
for eternity.

We have to remember, then, at the out-
set, these two things: (1) the simplicity
and purity, yet intense rationality, of Edwards's nature; and (2) the traditional faith,
which made all nature supernatural, that possessed and inspired him. From this point of
view the things that are most significant of

Edwards are not his deliberate and elaborate, but his most spontaneous, thoughts—those that came to him, as it were, by the way of intuition or meditation rather than by the method of logic and evidence. As indicating the quality of his nature, which is in a measure the hidden law of his mind, we may cite two things:

(1) Some of the resolutions he wrote before his nineteenth year:

" Resolved, Never to do any manner of thing, whether in soul or body, less or more, but what tends to the glory of God, nor be nor suffer it, if I can possibly avoid it.

" Resolved, to live with all my might, while I do live.

" Resolved, Never to do anything which I should be afraid to do if it were the last hour of my life.

" Resolved, Never to count that a prayer nor to let that pass as a prayer, nor that as a petition of a prayer, which is so made that I cannot hope that God will answer it."

The fine love of reality in the last resolution is specially noteworthy.

(2) This extract from his diary will show his innate mysticism, the degree in which he

was possessed of the passion for the divine;
"Once, as I rode out into the woods for my
health, in 1737, having alighted from my horse
in a retired place, as my manner commonly has
been, to walk for Divine contemplation and
prayer, I had a view, that for me was extra-
ordinary, of the glory of the Son of God, as
Mediator between God and man, and his wonderful, great, full, pure, and sweet grace and
love, and meek and gentle condescension. This
grace that appeared so calm and sweet appeared
also great above the heavens. The Person of
Christ appeared ineffably excellent, with an
excellency great enough to swallow up all
thought and conception—which continued, as
near as I can judge, about an hour; which
kept me the greater part of the time in a flood
of tears, and weeping aloud. I felt an ardency
of soul to be, what I know not otherwise how
to express, emptied and annihilated; to lie in
the dust and to be full of Christ alone; to
love him with a holy and pure love; to trust
in him; to live upon him; to serve and follow
him; and to be perfectly sanctified and made
pure, with a divine and heavenly purity. I
have several other times had views very much

of the same nature, and which have had the
same effects."

Let us now see how a man with so intense
and spiritual a nature as Edwards's, and yet so
speculative and rational a mind, possessed also
of a faith so intense and elevated, and so
completely isolated from the great intellectual
currents of the time—wrestled in thought with
its largest problems. We begin with some of
the positions that he lays down while quite a
young student as the result of his study of
Locke. Locke's analysis of the process of
knowledge led him to this—that the ultimate
source of ideas was sensation; that sensation
was due to the operation of external bodies,
and the quality which remained to the external
body in the ultimate analysis was Resistance,
which is only another form of Descartes's
Extension. But Edwards translates Locke's
resistance into a mode of divine energy or
will, thus : " There is nothing out of the mind
but Resistance, and as Resistance is nothing
else than the actual exertion of God's power,
so the power can be nothing else than the
constant Law or Method of that actual
exertion." Matter and energy are thus trans-

formed into the being and will of God ; and so
he again says : " Nor will it be found that the
principles we lay down at all make void natural
philosophy, or the science of the Causes or
Reasons of corporeal changes ; for to find out
the reasons of things, in natural philosophy, is
only to find out the proportion of God's acting."
He further thinks that all the natural changes
in the universe which follow in a continued
series " do not perhaps exist anywhere perfectly
but in the Divine Mind."   " But then, if it be
inquired, what exists in the Divine Mind ; and
how these things exist there ?   I answer, There
is his determination, his care, and his design,
that Ideas shall be united for ever, just so, and
in such a manner, as is agreeable to such a
series.   For instance, all the ideas that ever
were, or ever shall be to all eternity, in any
created mind, are answerable to the existence
of such a peculiar Atom in the beginning of
the Creation, of such a determinate figure and
size, and have such a motion given to it :
That is, they are all such as Infinite Wisdom
sees would follow according to the series of
nature, from such an Atom, so moved."

We here feel as if we were reading the first

and second books of Spinoza's "Ethics" through
the psychology of Locke as modified by Berkeley.
Edwards we may here term a monotheistic
idealist, with the emphasis on the *mono*. The
order of things we term nature is the order of
ideas in the mind of God, and this becomes our
order of ideas by the direct operation of the
creative mind. And so it follows that mind is
primary; indeed, in a sense there is nothing
but mind and its ideas, those of man being
effects from those of God. In words that
suggest Kant as well as Berkeley he says:
"*Place itself* is mental, and *Within* and *Without* are mere mental conceptions. . . . When
I say the Material Universe exists only in
the mind, I mean that it is absolutely dependent on the conception of the mind for its
existence, and does not exist as Spirits do,
whose existence does not consist in, nor in
dependence on, the conception of other minds.
. . . Things, as to God, exist from all Eternity,
alike; that is, the idea is always the same, and
after the same mode. The existence of things,
therefore, that are not actually in created
minds, consist only in Power, or in the Determination of God, that such and such ideas shall

11

be raised in creative minds, upon such conditions." He sums up his philosophical position
in these remarkable words (the italics are his
own) : "That which truly is the Substance of
all Bodies, is *the infinitely exact, and precise,
and perfectly stable Idea, in God's mind, together
with his stable Will, that the same shall gradually
be communicated to us, and to other minds,
according to certain fixed and exact established
Methods and Laws ;* or, in somewhat different
language, *the infinitely exact and precise Divine
Idea, together with an answerable, perfectly exact, precise, and stable Will, with respect to cor-
respondent communications to Created Minds,
and effects on their minds.*" * Nature thus becomes the continuous creation of God ; all our
knowledge is the result of His action, and in the
interpretation of what is without we are only

* Compare with the preceding and succeeding quota-
tions in the text the following propositions from Spinoza's
"Ethics": "Præter deum nulla dari neque concipi
potest substantia," "quicquid est, in Deo est, et nihil sine
Deo esse neque concipi potest." "Deus non tantum est
causa efficiens rerum existentiæ, sed etiam essentiæ." "In
rerum natura nullum datur contingens; sed omnia ex
necessitate divinæ naturæ determinata sunt ad certo modo
existendum et operandum." "Voluntas non potest vocari
causa libera, sed tantum necessaria." "Ordo et connexio
idearum idem est, ac ordo et connexio rerum."

really discovering the secret of what is within by thinking the thoughts of God after Him.

Let us see now how he works this fundamental idea out in his theology. And first as to his conception of Deity, which also involves that of the relation which He sustains to the universe. Edwards, then, formulates the principle that " God and real existence are the same ; God is, and there is none else." This is logically involved in his theory both of being and of knowing. For as real existence is ideal, the Divine as the fontal or creative mind is the source of all ideas, and is therefore the reality of all existence. And so he later expresses his notion thus : " The eternal and infinite Being is, in effect, being in general, and comprehends universal existence." And, again, he says : God is " the foundation and fountain of all being and all perfection, from whom all is perfectly derived, and on whom all is most absolutely and perfectly dependent ; whose being and beauty is, as it were, the sum and comprehension of all existence and excellence much more than the sun is the fountain and summary comprehension of all the light and brightness of the day." But as God is, such must the

creation be, for as is the fountain such is the
stream, as is the beginning such is the end.
And so he describes the end of the creation as
really contained within the Divine nature. "It
appears reasonable to suppose," he says, " that
it was God's last end that there might be a
glorious and abundant emanation of His infinite
fulness of good *ad extra,* or without Himself, and
that the disposition to communicate Himself, or
diffuse His own *Fulness,* was what moved Him
to create the world." As the end for which
the world was created is thus contained in
God, and as creation is "an emanation of His
own infinite fulness," it follows that as He is,
its end must be; and this end he describes in
twofold terms—as His own glory or as the
creature's good, but these as coincident and
identical, not as different, still less as opposed.
Thus he says: " God's respect to the creature's
good and His respect to Himself is not a divided
respect; but both are united in one, as the
happiness of the creature aimed at is happiness
in union with Himself." And again ; "Thus it
is easy to conceive how God should seek the
good of the creature, consisting in the creature's knowledge of holiness, and even his happi-

ness, from a supreme regard to *Himself;* as his happiness arises from that which is an image and participation of God's own beauty; and consists in the creature's exercising a supreme regard to God, and complacence in Him."

So far we have been concerned with his conception of God, and God's relation to the course and end of being; we have now to see how he translated his theology into religion. Religion was to him essentially imitation of God, the godly being the godlike man. As, then, God was, such ought the virtuous man to be. The methods and ends of the good were those of God. As to God, "he delights in his own goodness, and in the exercise of his goodness, and therefore he delights to make the creature happy, and delights to see him made happy." He says: "In God, the love of Himself and the love of the public are not to be distinguished as in man, because God's being, as it were, comprehends all." He means, then, that as man's obedience expresses God's perfection, the Divine glory is manifested in the character and the conduct of the saints, for "they are all but the emanations of God's glory, or the excellent brightness and fulness of the Divinity diffused, overflowing, and, as it were, enlarged; or, in one word, existing *ad extra*." Since religion is imitation of such a Deity, he conceives virtue "as love to the greatest happiness, or love to the happiness of universal being"; *i.e.*, the virtuous man is the man whose conduct is governed by the very end for which God made the world. For it is not merely personal happiness or love to our own personal pleasure which constitutes an action virtuous; on the contrary, he thus admirably distinguishes: "That which is often called *Self-love* is exceedingly improperly called *Love*, for they do not only say that one loves himself, when he sees something amiable in himself, the view of which begets delight. But merely an inclination to pleasure, and averseness to pain, they call Self-love: so that the devils and other damned spirits love themselves, not because they see anything in themselves which they imagine to be lovely, but merely because they do not incline to pain, but to pleasure." True virtue, therefore, "consists in love for God, the Being of Beings, infinitely the greatest and best." It is not the love of pleasure, but the happiness that is holiness—a certain kind of beautiful nature which appears in itself beautiful or comely because it so makes comeliness— is godlike because it tends to make the world like God.

While these are Edwards's fundamental and characteristic ideas, the heart as it were of his philosophy, they are modified in the working out by the formal logic and the imperfect psychology which he owed to Locke. When he turned from speculation to experience, he looked at it through the traditional beliefs of his people. These were, of course, embedded in the very speech of his community, the local conditions from which he could not extricate himself, as it were the vernacular into which he had been born. From this point of view we may regard the "Treatise on the Will" as not so much a creation of his philosophy as a theological inheritance; but its justification was altogether in his own manner. It is remarkable that while in his ultimate thinking he had so completely emancipated himself from empiricism, in this field of thought he identified himself with the school to which he was most radically opposed. For just as Collins had so developed Locke as to deny liberty and affirm necessity, and as Hume had resolved causation into mere antecedence and sequence, and as Henry Home had applied the same principles to the naturalistic explanation of morality and religion, so Edwards, in his "Treatise on the Will," turned his back upon his own philosophy and advocated one alien not only to Christianity, but even to theism. This may require a word of explanation. His fundamental notion that God is the only real cause may be made the basis of a theory of necessity, but then the necessity that it expresses will be one of universal benevolence. It may be quite victoriously argued that where God is the essence and energy of all that is, man cannot be free; but if God be conceived as so good as to will universal happiness, the ultimate end must be even as his will. It is remarkable that the thinker who had, on the most transcendental of all subjects, so broken with empiricism, should, at this point of transcendent practical importance, have fallen such a potent and willing victim to its exhausted charms. But we can see how it happened. The psychological basis of the Treatise Locke supplied. The will was identified with desire, choice with inclination. As desire always must be for the agreeable and towards the pleasant, so the will is always as the strongest motive is. Choice, in other words, was superseded by inclination, and where inclination or desire is the only form of choice the man is but the victim of circumstances, made according to what happens to him rather than according to what he is. The "Treatise on the Will" was Edwards's most elaborate work; it was also his most immediately influential. It was received in Scotland, to the dismay of his evangelical friends, with warm approval by their freethinking contemporaries. Henry Home and David Hume found their own ideas here expanded and enforced by the champion of the orthodox, and the latter, in dismay, turned to him for explanations of difficulties, which indeed he attempted to give even while he failed to perceive their real source and significance. We may leave the Treatise to its empirical admirers, while holding to the theology which is its corrective and negation.

Edwards was in many ways a man who exemplified the most characteristic qualities of New England. Occasionally, through his all too sombre speech, a kindly gleam of humour breaks. Thus he quaintly says, "Although the devil be exceedingly crafty and subtle, yet he is one of the greatest fools and blockheads in the world, as the subtlest of wicked men are. Sin is of such a nature that it strangely infatuates and stultifies the mind." Take him all in all, in the beauty of his character, in the elevation of his thought, his claim to stand amid the great thinkers of the world is indisputable. In England here we have just been making welcome the new edition of Bishop Butler's works —edited by the statesman who in his retirement shows his undiminished vigour and reveals his lifelong interest in theology—and I have been comparing Butler's answer to Tindal with Edwards's, with the result that I am forced to confess that while the rigour and vigour of inexorable logic and the strength which comes from a concentration due to the careful exclusion of all irrelevant matter are with Butler, the elevation, the insight, the oversight, the feeling of the magnitude of the problem, and the forecast of the lines along which the ultimate answer must move are all with Edwards. Still, he speaks to us in a strange tongue. It is, indeed, our mother speech, yet, as it were, in a dialect so remote from the culture of Europe, from the elegance of literature, and the discipline of the classics, that we hardly know it as our own; but when we have penetrated under the speech to the matter, and behind the form to the man, we are fain to confess that in this lone New Englander, preaching now in Northampton, whether amid the excitement of the Great Revival or in the face of the coldness of an estranged people, and now labouring in the backwoods at Stockbridge, amid Indians and amid countrymen ruder than the Indians, we yet have one who holds his place amid the most honourable of the doctors of the Church, of the philosophers of his century, and of the saints of God.

X.

HORACE BUSHNELL.

By the Rev.
T. T. MUNGER, D.D.

X.

HORACE BUSHNELL.

Horace Bushnell appeared at a time when a theologian was greatly needed in New England. The force of Edwards's influence had spent itself, or, rather, its soul had gone to feed an intellectual idealism, and its body had degenerated into a hard formalism. His overwhelming sense and assertion of God—a thing not easily brought within the limits of theology or philosophy as they are usually regarded—had lost its inspiring power.

When Dr. Bushnell began his ministry in Hartford in 1833, the churches may be said to have been living under a system rather than under truths. I will not use my limited space to enforce the distinction, though it is one of real importance. The good qualities that we ascribe to the churches of that day grew out of the truths involved in their theological system; their faults sprang out of their insistence that

those truths must be so defined and shaped as
to form a coherent system. It was a marvel
of exactness—definitions and proof-texts being
accepted—but it never satisfied the thinkers,
and was constantly being "improved." In its
last form it reposes in unpublished manuscripts
or unread volumes. But, though undergoing
constant modification, it was imposed on the
churches with relentless rigour as the substance
of their faith. Its conceptions of God and man
were alike defective, its exegesis was poor and
arbitrary, its logic formal and pedantic, and its
conclusions were often inhuman. While
involving great nourishing truths, it so combined them that they almost ceased to wear the
Christian cast. It is too well known to require
statement—a fall in Adam, who in some sense
contained or represented the race; a consequent
universal condemnation to eternal punishment;
an atonement that either endured the punishment or made some corresponding expression
of it; imputed sin and imputed righteousness;
electing grace and reprobation, each irrespective
of character except as it may have been anticipated in the counsels of eternity. Such, in
substance, was the theology that prevailed in

the early part of the century. As we now see
things, it interpreted hardly a fact pertaining
to God or man or Scripture or nature with
correctness, and yet it asserted dogmas that
presumed an exhaustive knowledge of them.
Great Biblical words like *faith* and *sacrifice* and
life were emptied of their real meaning and
made to carry a sense not intended. Texts
were taken out of their setting and used in
support of doctrines to which they do not refer ;
and thus the whole Bible was subordinated to
a system which only by a fiction could be
said to have its origin in it. It was mainly
designed to set forth the sovereignty and
the glory of God—in redemption indeed, but
the two terms were put in such a relation
that redemption was belittled by sovereignty
and actually failed in reflecting glory—a
mistake in the construction of the system
that has reacted fatally upon it. The mistake
was a natural one ; the idea of humanity and
of the scope of redemption had not yet fully
come.

Our reverence for the fathers leads us to
speak of the vanishing away of this system as
a change in habit of thought, but it is more

than that ; it is disappearing because it is no
longer regarded as true.

Important but not fundamental changes in it
were going on while Bushnell was a student in
Yale College.   The New Haven divines were
urging a view of the freedom of the will and
of the moral government of God which
developed a deeper sense of human responsibility and induced a revival of Christian activity
the effects of which were felt in the birth of
great religious enterprises that are still full of
power—an indication of emergence from the
prevailing theology.   But it was a period of
fierce controversy.   Dr. Taylor and Dr. Tyler
were dividing the churches over a metaphysical
notion of the will, the difference between them
being that one claimed that it was a little freer
than the other; and the degree of difference
was thought to involve results derogatory to
God and harmful to souls.   The condition,
intellectually and morally, was cluttered with
metaphysical distinctions, emanating from the
studies of men imperfectly educated, but keen
enough to see the lack of adjustment in a
system which showed such lack because it was
made up of truths which could not be dove-

tailed into each other. The pulpit was narrow and timid for fear of getting beyond the imposed conditions, or it was tyrannical in its insistence on them. The distinctions and differences had been growing since Edwards, and had reached a stage which Bushnell described in his preface to "Christ in Theology" as "the sedimentary subsidence of theology itself, precipitated in the confused mixture of its elements." Meanwhile in Massachusetts the Unitarian schism had paralysed Orthodoxy with fear, and no one dared to speak above one's breath. Professor Park had not yet come to Andover with his great word—one of the most effective ever spoken in the American pulpit—on "The Theology of the Intellect and the Feelings"—effective because it showed a way out of an over-rigid theology; a kind Providence provides such vents for intolerable beliefs.

What made this condition so deplorable, and so exasperating to Dr. Bushnell when he became a pastor, was that this system was carried into and imposed on religious experience. The Thirty-nine Articles are Calvinistic, but they are not intruded on the life of the Epis-

copal laity : wise but illogical. The clergy of
New England could not endure such inconsist-
ency.   Indeed, they had nothing to fall back on
if their dogmas were set aside ; they had no
function but to turn them into experience ;
the cardinal duty of the pulpit was to preach
them.   And well was it carried out—an
honest but doubtful business.   Religious experience was made to tally with the system and
run the round of its several members in a
fixed order.   Human life in all its complexity
and variety was forced to act under a sharply
defined conception of lost condition by nature,
heavy conviction of sin, struggle, surrender,
illumination by the Spirit, to be followed by
an experience of constant heart-searching with
possible doubts of election and never any
certainty of it, fear lest the sin against the
Holy Ghost had been committed, alternations of
peace and assurance with occasional ecstasies of
trust and hope ; but as a whole the experience
was overshadowed by morbid misgiving and
painful foreboding—a Puritan search for the
Holy Grail.

The experience was adjusted to a system,
every feature of which must be reproduced by

every person ; but while all were thus held
to the system with but small room for the
play of personal qualities, the experience was
absolutely individual : each soul was isolated
from every other, and almost from God, and
left to wrestle alone for salvation. This
emphasis upon system lay at the root of the
New England zeal for orthodoxy, and of its
intolerance of the slightest departure from it.
If one doubted any part, one doubted the whole.
If he doubted the eternity of punishment, he
endangered the moral government of God; if he
doubted decrees, all theology was involved in
confusion : both doubts were an impeachment
of the sovereignty of God.

Such was the condition of things when
Dr. Bushnell came upon the stage. Its main
feature was its unnaturalness. Each member
of the system represented or hinted at a truth,
but the truths were so defined and manipulated
that their real meaning evaporated and left
only a travesty of the Gospel. The system
bore little relation to human nature, took
no account of its variety or need, or method
of action, but loaded it with burdens which did
not belong to it, and then required it to throw

them off by processes that were arbitrary and unnatural.

Dr. Bushnell was reared and educated under this system, though some exceptional influences in childhood separated him somewhat from its more rigid features. He never broke away from it externally, but from the first he protested against it. He refused to think under it or along its lines, and the point of his stoutest protest was its unnaturalness. He took the path by which superior minds have always found their way into new realms of truth. They do not pass from one school to another, but instead rise into some new or some larger conception of nature and start afresh. All gains in philosophy and religion and civilisation have been made by farther inroads into nature, and never in any other way. Dr. Bushnell, with the unerring instinct of a discoverer, struck this path and kept it to the end. At the bottom of all his work lies a profound sense of nature, of its meaning and force in the realm of the spirit. He did not deny a certain antithesis between nature and the supernatural, but he so defined the latter that the two could be embraced in the one category of nature when

viewed as the ascertained order of God in creation. The supernatural is simply the realm of
freedom, and it is as natural as the physical
realm of necessity. Thus he not only got rid
of the traditional antinomy between them, but
led the way into that conception of the relation
of God to his world which more and more is
taking possession of modern thought. In his
essay on Language he says (and the thought is
always with him as a governing principle) :
" The whole universe of nature is a perfect
analogon of the whole universe of thought or
spirit. Therefore, as nature becomes truly a
universe only through science revealing its
universal laws, the true universe of thought
and spirit cannot sooner be conceived." Thus
he actually makes the revelation of spiritual
truth wait on the unfolding of the facts and
laws of the world of nature. There is something pathetic in the attitude of this great
thinker sitting in the dark, waiting for dis-
closures in nature that would substantiate what
he felt was true in the realm of the spirit. A
generation later he would have seen the light
for which he longed—a light that justifies the
central point of all his main contentions.

He seems to have taken to heart the fact
that God made the heavens and earth and all
that in them is. This sense of nature was
largely an endowment. No theologian was
ever more fully dowered with the seeing eye
and the interpreting mind. He was a poet
before he was a theologian, and his chief
excellence as the latter is due to his greatness
as the former. This Divine gift was stimulated
and directed by Coleridge, whose "Aids to
Reflection" kindled within him a passion for
thought and feeling early in his career. Thus,
without being fully aware of it, he was in close
accord with that modern habit of theological
thought which came in through Coleridge and
has since pervaded the theological world. Its
key is nature; its secret is reason. It sees
first and speculates afterward. Dr. Bushnell's
entire work may be characterised as a plea for
naturalness. His eye is always fixed on the
nature of things. His first book—"Christian
Nurture"—is a plea for Christian education
according to nature, as seen in the Divine
constitution of the family. "God in Christ"
and "Christ in Theology" are attempts to
bring the Trinity within conceptions that do

not violate nature. His Sabellianism grew out
of his desire to bring the Trinity under the
great principle of the Logos, and so get God
out of his incomprehensibility down into a
region where things are a revelation of God;
the Logos is the meeting-ground of God and
nature, the visible side of the invisible God. In
Christ God manifests himself as human, and
feels and acts and suffers in human ways, but it
is all Divine and yet natural as these processes
in man are natural.

"Nature and the Supernatural" had for its
purpose to include the two contrasted domains
within one category. The will itself, he
claimed, was a supernatural agent. "The
Vicarious Sacrifice" was an effort to state
the Atonement in terms that are justified in
human experience. His essays are careful
explorations into the nature and relations of
the thing under discussion; often they ran
wild with imagination, but in the farthest
flights he never let go of the guiding clue of
nature.

The times had much to do with the development and shaping of his powers. He began
his ministry just as that crisis was maturing

which ended the reign of superstition and tradition, and ushered in the scientific habit of
thought. It was a time well described in
Matthew Arnold's lines:

> Wandering between two worlds;
> One dead, the other powerless to be born.

Bushnell felt the deadness of one world, but
not the inability of the other to be born.
Born he at least would be, and his whole life
was one steady effort to find his way into this
new world where highest truths could be joined
to highest reason by the connecting bond of
nature. Nearly everything that he wrote was
grounded " in principles interpreted by human
analogies." The power and greatness of the
man lay in the fact that he was broad enough to
cover the world in which he first found himself,
and also that into which he made his way. He
did not abjure his past; he made no violent
break with the existing order; the weakness of
schism was not in him; he might be turned out,
but he would not himself go out. His historic
sense was strong, as it is with all great men, and
he shrank from violating it by external change.
The past contained great realities of faith and

practice, and he held fast to them. He had no liking for raw and violent denials and fresh-made doctrines. But while he held to the past, he played the part of critic with vigour, cleared it of its hardness and narrowness and supersti-tion, searched out "the soul of goodness" in it, and so paved the way into a world as new as that of which Arnold sadly dreamed.

I do not mean that Dr. Bushnell wholly parted with what now seem to us imperfect and provincial opinions in theology, nor that his thought was always what would now be regarded as scientific; no man ever wholly frees himself from the defects of his age; but he found his way into the world of the spirit. Instead of leaving one field and going over into another, he rose into a higher region that spanned both. The characteristic of the man was spirituality; his ruling passion was for freedom and order. He found his way into freedom along two paths—one by which he "passed into the vein of comprehensiveness, questioning whether all parties were not in reality standing for some one side or article of the truth"; the other was a theory of language which he regarded as his own peculiar work.

Whether it was a true theory or not it served
his purpose; if it was a hobby, it carried him
whither he was moved to go. His biographer
regards it as "the key to Horace Bushnell,"
and, undoubtedly, he is to be read under
his own theory of language. Its root is
to be found in the ancient doctrine of the
Logos. As used by himself, words became
the reflection of his thought rather than
"exact representatives" of it. This theory
seemed necessary to enable him to speak
according to his thought on such themes as
the Trinity, atonement, miracle, and regeneration—subjects that chiefly engaged his
attention. He found these great doctrines
tied up and smothered under hard and narrow
definitions. His first step was rejection of the
definitions; thus he escaped into the world of
the spirit, where language does not define but
only indicates or shadows forth. The chief
value of this theory of language lies in its
assertion that spiritual facts and processes
cannot be brought within strict definition.
We are getting to know this well enough
without a special theory. Possibly, however,
the day is not yet past when categorical

answers to sharply defined questions concerning infinite and eternal things are required of suspected teachers. In such a case a theory of language that eludes the dictum of "the evident meaning of the words" is not only convenient but justifiable, and is a proper defence when official bigotry worries such teachers. Even theology has its humorous side, and Samson may jest while the Philistines torture him. Dr. A——, his chief accuser, spends two days with Dr. Bushnell and is led to believe that there is no heresy in him; he could not understand his host's use of language.

I can but hint at the works which came from his prolific pen—a dozen volumes at least, five of them solid treatises on theology and the rest sermons or essays. There is a logical order in the treatises which indicates that one sprang out of or was rendered necessary by another. He began where theology has so often broken down and started afresh—as Dr. Prentice, of Union Seminary long ago pointed out—with children in a treatise on "Christian Nurture." It won all Christian motherhood and well-nigh the fathers, but it

190 HORACE BUSHNELL.

was discovered to be heretical, and charges
to that effect were brought, which never
relaxed but never accomplished anything
except to forward the doctrine they attacked.
The aim of the book was to establish the
proposition : " That the child is to grow up
a Christian and never know himself as being
otherwise "; a very simple statement but it
shook New England theology to its founda-
tions. It attacked the extreme individualism
into which theology had fallen, and recalled
it to those organic relations between parents
and children which are recognised in all the
historic Churches, and are steadily gaining
significance under modern thought. Christian
experience had become too supernatural; Dr.
Bushnell brought it within the range of human
nature. The effect of the treatise has been to
make Christian character not less a product
of Divine grace, and to reinforce it by the
natural relations of the family. Its main
idea is as old as the oldest religion; for no
men were ever so dull as to conceive or de-
velop a religion on a basis of pure individualism; but Dr. Bushnell treated the subject in
a full and thorough way, and prepared it for

the modern conceptions and applications of heredity.

The next book in point of influence is "The Vicarious Sacrifice." I refer only to the first volume, and not to the second, which was originally published under the title "Forgiveness and Law," and afterward incorporated with the first as a part of the same treatise. Its main purpose is to show that the object and issue of the atonement is the moral recovery of man. Christ did not die "to even up a score of penalty," but to make the cross a salvation by its power on life and character. The key to his view is found on the title-page: "The Vicarious Sacrifice, grounded in Principles of Universal Obligation." He regards "the sacrifice and cross of Christ his simple duty, and not any superlative, optional kind of good, outside of all the common principles of virtue. It is not goodness over good, and yielding a surplus of merit in that manner for us, but it is only just as good as it ought to be, or the highest law of right required it to be." Here again we detect the note of nature which is heard in all his writings. He will not admit that there is any principle or law in the atonement

which is not of "universal obligation." The
sacrifice of Christ meant and called for an
exactly corresponding sacrifice on the part of all
men; it *impressed* them for that end, and so
saved them. It is not penal, nor expiatory except
as it works morally to overcome evil, nor is it an
expedient to uphold a moral government. These
extra-human renderings of a simple and universal moral law are set aside to make room for
one that the twentieth century will hardly call
in question. No efforts to link this view with
those found in the old theologies—doubtless
it can be found in them—lessen its novelty as
it was propounded to the churches of New
England. As things were in 1866 it was
undoubtedly heretical, as many a sympathising
young pastor found to his cost. The volume
strengthened the suspicion awakened by
"Christian Nurture," and henceforth the
heresy connected with him was that of the
"moral view." Efforts were made to bring
him to trial, but the Congregational system
does not readily lend itself to such work, and
he suffered only such small penalties as the
religious newspapers inflicted, one of which
went into a decline under his stinging cha-

racterisation of it as "not only behind the age, but behind all ages." But he was not much given to controversy or self-defence. Only once or twice did he turn on his accusers, and then it was as with that "two-handed engine that smites once and smites no more." He was too profound a lover of truth to make it matter of debate; he did not so reach his conclusions, nor would he so defend them. He belonged rather to the order of seers, and simply declared what it had been given him to see, and so left it.

Whatever may be said of "The Vicarious Sacrifice" in the way of criticism, the fact remains that it introduced into New England theology the moral view of the atonement, and largely supplanted the existing view. The doctrine now preached in New England, with modifications indeed, and much of independent interpretation, is that which runs through this treatise—a fact recognised in a recent sermon by Professor George Harris, of Andover, in which he said that "his (Dr. Bushnell's) theory is now more generally accepted than any other."

This theory runs through all his books. It

13

was infolded in his first work—"Christian
Nurture"—which, indeed, contained the germ
of all his writings. This was inevitable. When
he struck out the great truth that the Christian
training of a child must be in the ways of
nature, nature being regarded as God's order,
it was inevitable that every doctrine and phase
of Christian truth should be treated in like
manner. Dr. Bushnell early, and by the very
quality of his nature, fell into the scientific
habit of thought, and he kept to it throughout.
He was often mystical, sometimes inconsistent,
but at bottom, in all his conceptions and in
almost every sentence, he was scientific; that
is, he kept his eye on facts, on the things that
are made, on the divine order wrought into the
nature of man, and reasoned from them. Therefore, when he came to treat of miracles—an
inevitable theme for 'him—he searched and
enlarged the realm of nature to find a place for
them. Here again his thought may be at times
inaccurate, and without the severity that would
now be insisted on, but none the less did he
redeem the subject from definitions and inter-
pretations that defied reason and provoked
unbelief. He did more; he directed attention

to the field where they must be located, and
stated the general principles under which they
must be regarded; he broke down the artificial
barrier between two worlds which are not two
but one, and made us see that unity in the works
of God which destroys the antithesis between
nature and miracle, and brings all into one
spiritual category. The purpose of the book is
indicated in its title : "Nature and the Supernatural as together Constituting the One System
of God." The treatise is still of great value,
and is perhaps the best on the subject. The
tenth chapter has become a Christian classic.
The writer did not have the advantages afforded
by recent science. Evolution, which simplifies
the treatment of all subjects, was nothing more
than a disputed hypothesis; biology was a new
science ; the new psychology was in its infancy,
and exegesis was still enthralled under a hard
and narrow doctrine of inspiration. The
limitations of the treatise are due to these
conditions, but all the more does it reveal the
bravery and insight of the author; he anticipated discoveries and wrought the spirit of them
into his pages. He hewed out a path through a
very tangled wilderness, guided only by his

insight into the things of God and by a deep
sense of the need of finding a way through.
The condition in which the subject lay when
Dr. Bushnell began to write was lamentable; it
was exactly that reprobated by Christ when the
Jews clamoured for a sign. Thus preached, it
played fatally into the hands of infidelity, and
added to the perplexity of a faith that was
already heavily burdened. As on other subjects, he opened a way out, stemming the tide
of schismatic denial and rejection by leading
men into a region where they could at least
think with some show of reason, and look about
them with their feet planted on the nature of
things. Dr. Bushnell was accounted a heretic,
but he saved orthodoxy, at least what of it was
worth saving. The churches of New England
were fast drifting into a condition where schism
or dry-rot would have soon made an end of them.
He arrested this process, and rediscovered for
them the world of the spirit; he directed their
attention to the nature of things, and made
them a logos of Divine truths; he created a soil
for an ethical and reasonable faith, and sowed
seed in it that is still yielding ever-increasing
harvests.

The recognition of his service was tardy and scant except among the younger clergy. There was, however, a quasi-recognition in the distinction that was made between his sermons and his treatises; the latter were generally set down as dangerous, but the former were acknowledged to be full of spiritual power and comfort. The distinction but showed the pitiful state of criticism at the time; it was kind but weak. The sermons and the treatises grew out of each other, and were but forms of the same thing. But lack of recognition is a trifling matter; the true prophet is aware that it must be so. It was not a specially sore thing to Dr. Bushnell. He was immensely stored with inner resources. He delighted in his own thoughts, and he found his way into that hidden world where he "fed on God" (his own phrase), and so had strength and health of soul. Late in life he said to a friend, "I have been greatly blessed in my doubtings." In New England, and not less in Great Britain, a more Christ-like Gospel is preached, and Christian believers the world over are living in the exercise and comfort of a more rational faith, because of the work he did.

He was a solitary thinker. His writings lack
the signs of full contact with the scholastic
world ; and perhaps they are all the better for
it. They suggest by their style and form that
he thought as he wrote, and that he worked his
way along to his conclusions instead of starting
with a full plan. Hence he often found it
necessary to qualify and correct what he had
said, and so his writings have a prolixity that
might have been avoided.

The real greatness of Bushnell does not consist in his strictly theological work, but in those
separate and yet connected spiritual revelations
in which his life abounded. Read his books
—treatise or essay or sermon—and it is not
the truth of thought that most impresses you,
but the truth of experience. He was pre-
eminently a thinker, but he was still more a
practical man in the realm of the spirit. A
man of affairs, of keen worldly insight and
wisdom, he carried this quality into the things
of the spirit. He had no " unrelated facts,"
as every title-page and every chapter shows.
His apprehension of God in his personal
experience, the play of his own spirit back and
forth in God, his moral interpretation of life

and of history, his ready perception of the divinest truths in his daily walks, his easy and natural lifting of the earthly into the heavenly, and bringing the powers of eternity down into the commonest events of life—these things constitute the greatness and power of the man. In his life as well as in his writings he overcame the dualism he found in the prevailing theology, and became himself a revelation of the oneness of God in the world of the spirit and in nature.

The limits of this article permit no mention of Dr. Bushnell as a preacher, nor of the varied work which he performed in other fields than theology, nor of the incidents of his life. I cannot spread out in detail his character, in which virility, mental vigour, saintliness, common sense, imagination, and spiritual insight waged no war with one another, but instead conspired to produce a man who stands on the same plane with Edwards and Channing and Emerson—the other great teachers of the spirit whom New England has produced.

XI.

FREDERICK DENISON MAURICE.

By the Rev.
A. V. G. ALLEN, D.D.

XI.

FREDERICK DENISON MAURICE.

THERE are some voices which are impersonal,
speaking, as it were, out of the darkness, giving
no hint of time or place, and gaining nothing
in power or directness by a study of their
environment. Such was Thomas à Kempis,
whose message comes with equal force to every
age. Something of this quality was in Maurice,
imparting to his thought a certain enduring
appeal, as if he belonged to no particular time
or country, or had received no special influence
from his surroundings. And yet no man ever
lived more deeply in the heart of his generation,
and his teaching contains a profound response
to the immediate needs of the hour.

The world into which he entered seemed
to be losing its hold on God. Among his
more eminent contemporaries Carlyle com-
plained that God was doing nothing ; Mill
regarded the Divine existence as an open ques-

tion, and Darwin appeared to have lost his
religious faculty. It was a world interested
in reform, whose watchwords were liberalism
and progress, whose programme called for the
removal of ancient abuses, under which were
included religion and the Church. In the
place of these relics of a bygone age, science
was offered and the religion of humanity, as if
adequate substitutes. Agitations were rife for
the improvement of social conditions; but the
leaders, for the most part, had ceased to look
to God for aid or inspiration—it was time at
last that men should help themselves. The
labouring men, with their grievances, turned
away from the Church and the means of grace
as if they were empty mockeries. The higher
walks of thought and culture were invaded
with religious doubt, a mood in which men
would fain believe but could not. The negation had gone deeper than in the eighteenth
century, when men professed, at least, to
believe in natural religion, and when on this
ground Bishop Butler had met them with his
Analogy. Now natural religion was called in
question ; it had become the issue whether God
existed or the soul of man was immortal.

Efforts were not wanting to meet the situation
—proposed reconstructions of the Church after
antique models which had once been useful, or
the presentation of the claims of the Roman
Church as somehow strangely adapted to the
requirements of the hour.

These were the problems of the age to which
Maurice appealed with the conviction that "no
man," as he had said of Coleridge, "will ever
be of much use to his generation who does not
apply himself mainly to the questions which
are agitating those who belong to it." It was
the burden of his message that God was mani-
festing himself in the contemporary world of
human thought and activity. "The knowledge of God," he wrote, "I regarded as the
key to all other knowledge, as that which connected knowledge with life." And again, "The
only way to consider philosophy is in connection with the life of the world, and not as a
set of merely intellectual speculations and systems." The light of the world was first revealed in life, and life was the light of men.

The preparation of Maurice for his mission
as a theologian began in his early years, as a
child in the household. His father was a Uni-

tarian minister, with a simple, genial creed
whose principal tenet was the fatherhood of
God; his mother was a Calvinist, thinking of
God as absolute sovereign will without whose
decree of election salvation was impossible, and
for herself doubting if her name were enrolled
among the elect. Maurice was forced by his
filial love and respect, no less than by his
sympathetic nature, but also by his spiritual
insight, to live in the creed of both his parents,
and was thus early called to mediate between
religious attitudes that seemed to neutralise
each other.

His method of solving the difficulty was a
simple one. He insisted that both creeds
should be understood as expressing realities or
existing relationships, not merely analogies of
human reasoning or notions of the mind which
it was pleased to entertain. When thus
interpreted, the reconciliation followed—the
absolute Sovereign of the universe, whose will
was inflexible, was at the same time the Infinite
Father whose love was the inmost essence of
his being. If no one could escape from the
control of absolute and sovereign Will, so also
no one could be excluded from the love of the

Eternal Father. The range of fatherhood was
co-extensive with the energy of the Divine will.
It expanded before the vision till it included
not only the Church but the whole secular
world as well.   Maurice admitted no distinction between a special and a common grace, for
such a distinction was incompatible with the
idea of fatherhood.   Preterition or reprobation
as defined in the language of the schools were
not fit expressions for describing the economy
of the Divine will, which was also a father's
love.   Everywhere it was the same God, call
him the Infinite Father or the sovereign Will,
who condemned the evil and inspired the good.
The loving providence or the infinite purpose
of existence must therefore be revealed in every
sphere of human life, in the Church and in
religion, but also in philosophy and literature,
in art and science, in politics and in the social
order.

But, further, the relationship of God to the
world, since it was an actual or real relationship and not a notion begotten by the mind,
must still exist apart from and despite its
latency to the consciousness. The energising of
the Divine will was not dependent upon human

acknowledgment nor limited in its activity by
human recognition.   The fatherhood of God.
embracing in its scope every child of man, was
the latent reality which gave significance to
baptism or invested with a deeper meaning the
process of conversion. If there were danger
that the doctrine of the Divine fatherhood might
be misinterpreted to sanction laxity or indulgence, yet, when conjoined in organic unity
with sovereign will, the love of God became the
supreme principle of moral law ; righteousness
was seen as the inmost essence of the loving
purpose which has gone forth into creation ;
the fatherhood which demanded righteousness
in the children could grant no relaxation, but
must seek and surely find its accomplishment
through manifold agencies in life, through
chastisement or the bitter agony of experience
whether in this world or in another. If the
moral purpose of God does not always appear in
direct manifestation, yet indirectly it never fails
to be revealed in the confusion and misery which
await the infringement of the moral law. The
existence of evil was the one subject upon which
Maurice refused to speculate.   But while he did
not inquire why sin should have entered the

world, he dwelt upon the experience that condemned it—how the Bible, the Church, society, and each individual conscience bore witness to its ravages. He recognised also that the normal order of the world and the constitution of man were visibly at war with evil, and since the Divine love was revealed in the constitution of things, and was also identical with sovereign will, evil must at last be overcome and banished from the universe.

It fell to the lot of Maurice to come into close personal contact with almost every variety of religious thought in England; and, by virtue of that mysterious element in his personality which made him from his childhood a mediator in religious differences, he learned to live, as it were, in the divergent forms of the common household of faith, to feed upon the truth they held, so that he could interpret their mission from within their fold. In this way he accepted the doctrine of the "inner light" as held by the Quakers, while clinging also to the necessity of sacraments and outward form as revealed in the spiritual life of organic historic Christendom. He was thrown among the Irvingites, and listened to their urgent cry for

14

the living Spirit who once wrought by signs
and wonders in the Apostolic age. But he
could not believe that the Spirit's action was
shut up to any one form of manifestation or
that it had ever been withdrawn from the
Church. The Holy Spirit appeared to him as
the actually existing bond of every unity,
whether domestic or social or ecclesiastical, a
spirit which united men by bringing them into
the fellowship of the Father and the Son;
which spake by the prophets, but also in the
conscience and higher reason of every man;
who inspired the writers of the sacred books,
but a Spirit also without whose constant
presence and inspiration no man could think or
perform those things that are good. Through
his connection with the evangelical churches
Maurice learned to identify the Gospel of Christ
with the proclamation of a message of deliverance from sin and guilt. He remained at heart
an Evangelical all his days, but he also widened
the range of Christ's redemptive work, till it
included all other deliverances, from every form
of oppression and tyranny, whether ecclesiastical, political, or social. In all this Maurice
may appear as the pioneer in some method

unknown before. But one is also impressed
with that unbroken chain of spiritual influence
by which the generations are bound together,
handing on to those who follow the truth
which has been received, waiting only till
God shall provide the medium, the fitting soil
in which the living seed at last shall germinate,
take root, and spring upward and bring forth
fruit an hundred fold.

In his intellectual development Maurice had
the unusual advantage of taking the full course
of study at Oxford first, and then at Cambridge. He caught the spirit, the subtle
quality of each of the great Universities which
have stood throughout their history for differ-
ing ideals and tendencies in English thought.
Cambridge has been the congenial home of
spiritual largeness and freedom. There Puritanism found its stronghold in the sixteenth
century, to be followed by the liberal school in
the English Church of Cudworth, More, and
Whichcote. It was at Cambridge that the
Evangelical School was nourished, and to Cambridge belongs the honour of ranking Coleridge
among its pupils. Oxford, on the other hand,
which in the Middle Ages was more closely

identified with the scholastic philosophy, has
given birth to two great Conservative movements, the Anglican revival under Laud in the
seventeenth century, and again under Newman
and Pusey, of which the tendency in both cases
was to idealise or deify the existing institution
as against the disintegrating forces of change or
revolution. Maurice felt the historical appeal,
the sense of historical continuity which Oxford
cherishes, but the influence of Cambridge was
the stronger. He imbibed there what may be
called the spirit of Platonic realism, according
to which the eternal idea or pattern of human
things is always larger than its embodiment in
any human institution and for ever calls men to
rise to its fuller appreciation. However vision-
ary or impracticable the idea may seem, its
deepest ground is invoked in the Eternal Will.
Thus Maurice was led to insist upon the ideal
constitution of the Church in Christ its head,
as the actual reality, and not a mere spiritual
aspiration which could rest in the background
of thought. His conception of the Church,
which brought him into conflict with what may
be called an Aristotelian realism, divinising the
existing order as if change or improvement

were but sacrilege, was throughout his life one
of the ruling ideas of Maurice's theology. He
preached it to the working-men, he traced its
presence in history, he urged it as the basis of
Christian unity, he would have it carried to the
heathen world as the solvent of its dark confusion—the brotherhood of human souls, a
divine-human fellowship of which Christ was
the head and leader, the Holy Spirit the bond
of inward unity, the fatherhood of God its
eternal ground in the infinite and sovereign
will.

The man who wrought most powerfully upon
Maurice after leaving the university was Coleridge, "the Master," as he has been called,
" of those who know."   Maurice did not come
into personal contact with him, but the study
of his life and his writings reconciled him to
the Church of England, of which he became a
minister, and, above all, taught him the significance of the doctrine of the Trinity.   It was no
longer an arithmetical puzzle as it had seemed
to the typical mind of the last century, but the
comprehensive formula of the Christian faith,
which contained the reconciliation of the con-
tradictions of speculative thought about the

Divine existence as well as the satisfaction of
the deeper needs of the spiritual life. In the
light of God as one and yet triune, the fellowships and relationships of earth were disclosed
as having their ground and justification in the
eternal fellowship which existed in the bosom of
God. In this conviction the Christian Church had
resisted the pressure of the imperial will in the
ancient days of its alliance with the Roman
Empire—that the Son of God who had
assumed humanity in the body of this flesh
was one and co-equal with the Father. And
again in the strength of this conviction, the
barbarism which overcame the Empire had in
turn been overcome. It had also been the
watchword of Christianity in the struggle with
Islam when the seemingly difficult and complex
idea of God had triumphed over a seeming
simplicity, which was, after all, but an empty
abstraction. But its historical interest and
significance paled before its spiritual and moral
appeal to the individual soul, or to social
reformers rejecting the Church and disowning
God. For the deep-seated and widespread
scepticism of the age was assuming that God
existed apart from human life, indifferent to

human suffering, enforcing obligations and
calling for sacrifices with which in Deity there
could be no sympathy, for they were alien to
the Divine nature.   But, in the name of God as
Father, Son, and Holy Ghost, human relationships and duties and obligations of self-sacrifice
were taken up, as it were, into God, and glori-
fied by His inmost essential life.   The Divine
became the prototype of the human;   eternal
fatherhood and sonship were the pattern from
which the human relationship was derived, and
not an analogy inferred from the human family.
Sacrifice and suffering entered as an integral
factor into the Divine life, before it proceeded
forth from God as the moral law of the universe.
In the incarnation of God in Christ and in the
atoning sacrifice on the cross was illustrated the
identification of Divine with human interests.

So great was the importance which Maurice
attached to the doctrine of the triune name that
in his book on "The Religions of the World"
he applied it as a test by which they were to
be measured and judged. Confucianism and
Mohammedanism could not rise to the truth
of the fatherhood of God because they lacked
the knowledge of the Son, through whom alone

fatherhood could be fully revealed. Brahminism
abounded in incarnations of the Divine, but they
ended in themselves because the knowledge was
wanting of the Eternal Father. Buddhism
dreamed of an infinite Spirit in which all men
shared, but because it did not know the Father
and the Son its doctrine of the Spirit was void,
as its highest goal was also reduced to Nirvana.

The ample learning which Maurice needed in
order to illustrate and enforce the truth which
he discerned, he had the opportunity to gain
during the years from 1840 to 1853, when he
held the professorship of history and literature
in King's College in London. His books bear
witness, and more particularly his "History of
Philosophy" and his "Social Morality," to the
thoroughness and depth of his acquaintance
with systems of thought, or his insight into
men and motives, or his power of interpreting
literature and life. In these works we may
read his appeal to the educated mind of his age.
He does not offer new arguments for the Divine
existence, or endeavour to overcome scepticism
by dialectics, but rather makes manifest how
God is revealed in all the higher forms of
human thought and expression. All history

resolved itself before his eyes into a spiritual
drama. The world everywhere appeared to him
as bearing witness to God, as if it were fed with
the life of God and shone with the light of
God. But Maurice does not appear in his books
or elsewhere in his work as if engaged or pre-
occupied with the anxious search for God. If
he seems burdened, it is as if the weight of the
Divine revelation might overpower him. His
attitude is that of receptivity for truth, or as if
passivity were the condition for seeing and
receiving.   His   experience   confirms   what
Wordsworth had taught:

> Nor less I deem that there are powers
>   Which of themselves our minds impress;
> That we can feel this mind of ours
>   In a wise passiveness.
>
> Think you 'mid all this mighty sum
>   Of things for ever speaking,
> That nothing of itself will come,
>   But we must still be seeking.

In addition to his other work, Maurice gave
much of his time and thought to the improvement of the working classes. So identified was
he with the cause of social reform that he
became known as the father of Christian

Socialism.   He was the founder of a college for
working-men whose success was mainly owing
to his disinterested labours.   He had a lofty
conception of the capacity of men engaged in
physical toil and without education to receive
the higher forms of truth and the results of
learning.   He aimed to overcome their peculiar
scepticism as to whether God were doing anything for the emancipation of society from
its oppression.   It was the spirit of his teaching
that it was God who was raising up the very
reformers who disowned Him, that it was a
Divine Spirit which stirred up social discontent
as the condition of social progress.

While the thought of Maurice does not lend
itself easily to brief summaries, yet it is not
difficult to trace in all his writings one common
element which binds them together in a con-
sistent whole.   That " religious realism " which
enabled him to grasp the fatherhood of God
as an actual relationship which could not be
broken may be discerned in every attitude of
his mind.   He looked upon religious institu-
tions, not as identical with their Divine idea,
but as witnesses to a higher reality.   Because
the reality existed independently of its acknow-

ledgment, he could be charitable while holding
the strongest convictions, dogmatic while re-
joicing in the largest freedom of thought.
What to the popular mind seemed like Divine
indifference to human affairs was to his mind
the visible token of His presence. The religious
doubt from which others fled in alarm, he
welcomed as an aid to the deeper knowledge of
God. Where others spoke of a lost and ruined
world, he spoke of a world which had been
redeemed by Christ. Some said that only
those who had been baptized were the children
of God; others, that to become a child of God
one must have been converted and have the
witness of an inward experience; he said that
all men were children of God in virtue of their
creation by the Eternal Father. Against those
who maintained that religion was repugnant
to the natural man, he affirmed religion to
be that which the heart needed and for
which it craved. In contrast with the method
of those who laboured to overcome the natural
depravity of the heart as the first step in
religious experience, he preached the "God
within," even to reprobates, as a Divine appeal
in order that they might claim the heritage of

sonship. In the common thought the Church of God was identified with some existing institution; he regarded the institution as witnessing to the existence of the Church. The true Church did not require to be founded or carried, but to be proclaimed as having already an actual existence, the brotherhood of men in Christ. It was customary in speaking of the forms of human government to classify theocracy by itself, as if it had once existed among the Jewish people or been attempted as an experiment at various moments in history; but he maintained that theocracy, God's government, underlay all forms of human government as their pattern, the test by which they would be vindicated or condemned.

This reversal of ordinary judgments, to which men have become accustomed by long habit of training, constitutes a difficulty in reading Maurice which is not easily overcome —a difficulty akin to that which followed the Copernican discovery, when reality was placed in such strange contradiction to the testimony of the senses that it still requires an effort of the mind to adjust the seeming appearance with the actual fact. There was one inference

which Maurice urged with great strenuous-
ness—that in the spiritual world relationships
were timeless, or could not be expressed in
terms of quantity; that eternal life and eternal
death were phrases charged with spiritual
potency without reference to their duration.
This contention regarding the use of the
word "eternal" goes to the heart of the
Maurician theology, affording a glimpse into
a higher order, where things are not what
they seem; where, instead of the Divine re-
volving around the human, God becomes the
central sun of an infinite spiritual universe
in whom men live and move and have their
being. The relationship of fatherhood and
sonship constitutes the law of spiritual gravi-
tation from which there is no escape, in
whose glad recognition and obedience consists
eternal salvation.

But, apart from his theological teaching, it
is the supreme tribute to be paid to Maurice
that he stood throughout his life as a con-
fessor to his age, listening to the story of
human doubt in deep sympathy, and never
turning his ear away from any man who found
difficulty in believing. Tennyson, who was his

friend, has described him in what he did for
himself and for others:

The faith, the vigour, bold to dwell
  On doubts that drive the coward back,
  And keen through wordy snares to track
Suggestion to her inmost cell.

He fought his doubts and gathered strength,
  He would not make his judgments blind,
  He faced the spectres of his mind
And laid them; thus he came at length

To find a stronger faith his own;
  And power was with him in the night,
  Which makes the darkness and the light,
And dwells not in the light alone.

It was the testimony of Archdeacon Hare,
while Maurice was still alive, that no one had
done so much in reconciling the reason and
the conscience of the thoughtful men of the
age to the faith of the Church: "It is in great
measure owing to him that the intellect of the
rising generation is with us rather than against
us." In the words of another eminent contemporary, Dr. Montagu Butler: "Wherever rich
and poor are brought closer together, wherever
men learn to think more worthily of God in
Christ, the great work that he has laboured

at for nearly fifty years shall be spoken of as a memorial of him." He held no high preferment in the Church of England, but the world recognised him for what he was and for what he had done. At his death in 1872 there was a demonstration of public feeling which for spontaneity and universality had not been witnessed since the funeral of the Duke of Wellington. Beneath his bust in Westminster Abbey is recorded the only estimate we need: "He was not that light; but was sent to bear witness of that light."

XII.

CAN WE BE PROPHETS?

By the Very Rev.
F. W. FARRAR, D.D.

XII.

CAN WE BE PROPHETS?

1. Can we be prophets? Most assuredly, yes. It is not the possibility which is wanting, but the will. We are called to be, every one of us in our degree and measure, prophets of the Lord; interpreters, that is, of His will to men, both on our lips and in our lives. It is, then, most important to us to meditate and understand what a prophet is, what he has to do, what he has to expect, what he may hope to achieve. What the prophet has to do is to sweeten the moral air which the world breathes; to raise the tone of society; to expose the hollowness of the compromises which the heart is constantly making with the powers of evil; to set forth an example of "something higher and more heroical in religion than his age affects"; to turn men's eyes from the dancing bubbles of avarice and ambition to the distant, the future, and the unseen; to live as one

to whom it has been granted to see the things that are invisible. This inscription was found carved over a temple door in a southern island: "The world was given us for our own upbuilding, not for the purpose of raising sumptuous houses; life, for the discharge of moral and religious duties, not for pleasurable indulgence; wealth, to be liberally bestowed, not avariciously hoarded; learning, to produce good actions, not empty disputes." In other words, life is a serious and noble thing, and we are in daily danger—a danger to which most of us succumb—of making it a paltry, a petty, a frivolous, a dishonest, and a corrupted thing. And if God sends us prophets, it is that they may raise us up; that their words and deeds may breathe like a fresh wind through the perfumed and polluted atmosphere of society; that they may become electric to flash through all the world the wholesome lightnings of truth and faith, startling the strongholds of immoral selfishness and shattering the refuges of accepted lies. And yet all this the prophet has to do, often alone; often in deep obscurity and isolation; often in the midst of poverty and persecution; and he must do it with a deep and crushing sense of his own feebleness and imperfections, but making a loyal sacrifice of his earthly life and his earthly hopes. How, then, can we be prophets—we, the worldly; we, the sensual; we, the idle and sluggish; we, the vulgar and conventional; we, who worship Mammon, and love pleasure, and delight so much in scandal and hatred and lies? As we are, we cannot be prophets; but are the wings of six-winged seraphim—the twain with which they did fly—folded for ever? Is there no temple more? Is heaven closed for ever? Burns there no fire on the altar? Has the chariot of heaven ceased to descend to earth? Are there no hot coals of fire to touch and purify the unclean lips? Does the Lord say no longer from His throne above the cherubim, "Whom shall I send, and who will go for us?" He who made the stammerer Moses His lawgiver, when he was but a shepherd of alien sheep in the wilderness; He who made the peasant Amos a prophet, as he earned his few daily pence by gathering the coarse fruit of the sycamore ; He who made a prophet of Jeremiah when he was yet but a timid child; He who slung a sword round the neck of the least

of the children of Manasseh, and sent him forth
to smite the innumerable foe—cannot He make
sons of God and heroes of us, even of us ? If
the world summoned us to her splendours and
her feasts, if some one offered us a life of ease
and wealthy self-indulgence, what a rush there
would be to claim it !

> Hark ! rising to the ignoble call
> How answers each bold Bacchanal !

But when God calls us and offers Heaven as
the issue, will we all slink back in silence ?
Shall He alone find none to brave sorrow and
loss for Him, among the many whom He has
made ?   Well, He calls us now !

2. But God never deceives us.   His prophets
must be made of stern stuff, men of nerve and
insight.   He does not promise us any primrose
path of dalliance.   He says, " If ye would be
my soldiers, ye must endure hardness.   If ye
would run in my race, ye must train.   If ye
would be my athletes, ye must deny yourselves.
If ye are to be my prophets, then, like all my
best and greatest prophets, in the world ye
shall have tribulation."   Why must this be so ?
It is, in one word, because the prophet must

escape the average. The mass of mankind live the average life. They are easy-going, conventional, traditional, commonplace. They do what others do; say what others say. They do not either think or act for themselves; any shibboleth does for them, so that it is current; any sophism suffices them, so it be accepted; they are but echoes; they pair off, as one has said, in insane parties, and because they ignore the deep realities of morals and religion, they detest to have their sand-built houses shaken, or their sluggish ease disturbed. It is almost incredible how hostile mankind has been to its greatest men. Scarcely ever has there been a great soul uttering truth but there has been the shadow of Calvary. It is because the majority do not like trouble; and to face new truth is a trouble. However much they may be told that there is no such word as *mumpimus*, still, like the old Catholic priest, they will refuse to change it for the right but unfamiliar *sumpsimus*. And that is why the world poisons Socrates, who bids it think out its own philosophy, and burns those who bid it amend its false religion. Majorities are constantly in the wrong. When Phocion heard the multitude

applaud his speech, he turned round in surprise and asked, "Have I said anything wrong,
then?" "Always," as Goethe said, "it is the
individual who works for progress, not the age.
The ages have always been the same." It is
this fact which robs of any cynical bitterness
the saying of a great writer, that the world is
composed of some thousand million human
beings—mostly fools. Well, but the prophet
must escape the average; he must not be a fool.
Least of all must he be so in spiritual intuition
and moral views.

3. Now, we cannot get to practical applications till we have grasped fundamental facts;
we cannot do even small duties without the
strength inspired by great principles. It
requires a converted character to make even
a thoroughly honest and satisfactory house-
maid. It is not so easy as men generally assume
to be a Christian. To be a party religionist—to
be an Evangelical, or a Broad Churchman, or a
High Churchman—is very easy. But it is not
easy to be a brave, true, honest man. Let me,
then, try to illustrate what I have been saying.
Let me try to show that no man can be truly
good unless he escapes the average; to show

that to escape the average costs something; and so, gradually, from great examples, to learn what to us is so inestimably precious and indispensable to learn; namely, how—with some courage and some insight—to do our duty. Would God all the Lord's people were prophets; but we cannot be so by echoing common falsehoods and by running in conventional grooves. Let me show, by an instance, what the prophet must do and bear.

4. In the third century after Christ a boy was born at Alexandria, of Christian parents, in days of persecution. His parents trained him carefully, and he showed, even as a child, so bright a wisdom that, as he slept, the father would sometimes kiss reverently the breast of his sleeping son, whom he regarded as a temple of the Holy Ghost. Fierce persecution arose, and the father was seized and imprisoned. The boy, then but sixteen years old, showed such ardent longing for the crown of martyrdom that his mother had to conceal his clothes, and so prevent him from going forth into peril; yet, even then, he wrote to his father to be brave and not to shrink. The father was martyred. The boy, left with a mother and five

brothers and sisters entirely destitute, toiled for their support. Being a prodigy of learning, he supported himself by teaching pupils, and then sold all his books of classic literature for an annuity of a few pence a day, on which, throughout life, he lived. Taking the Gospel literally, he would have no shoes, and but one coat, and would touch no strong drink, and lived from boyhood in severe and noble simplicity. Almost before he was a man he became the head of the great catechetical school of Alexandria. Amid constant perils he lived a life which was, from first to last, one long prayer, one long struggle for closer union with the Eternal and the Unseen. He exercised on the Church of his own day, and of all succeeding ages, an almost incredible influence. He had saints and martyrs and holy hermits and wise bishops among his converts and pupils. He won over to the faith alike Christian heretics and heathen philosophers. He wrote hundreds of books and pamphlets which others, without acknowledgment, appropriated. He was, even by the confession of his enemies, the greatest man who had risen in the Church since the days of the Apostles, and perhaps also the

holiest.   His homilies have been the type of all
homilies since.   He laid the very foundation of
the science of textual criticism.   He was the
first who attempted a philosophy of Christianity.
After years of incredible labour and self-denial,
in which he rendered to the Church such services as no man has ever rendered since, he
died a martyr's death in the Decian persecution.
That man was the great Christian Father,
Origen the Adamantine.   And what was his
reward?   In his lifetime, bitter envy, malignant
persecution; after his death, the *damnamus* of
Augsburg and the *anathema* of Rome.   The
splendour of his attainments raised him a host
of enemies; the depth of his thoughts frightened
the conventional ignorance which took itself for
Orthodox belief.   This greatest and holiest of
men was branded as a heretic nearly three centuries after his death by the combined intrigues
of a cunning and worthless bishop and a cruel
emperor.   For centuries it continued to be
debated whether he was not suffering infernal
torments; and though, in the fifteenth century,
when learning revived once more, and a ray of
light out of God's eternity woke the Middle
Ages from their dark and ghastly dream, when

ancient Greece once more "started into life, but
with the New Testament in her hand"—though,
I say, since then the best and greatest have ever
honoured the name of Origen, yet this is the
man at whom, to this day, every raw sciolist
and every full-fed Pharisee still thinks that he
may cast a stone. Why? Because Origen was
a prophet; he escaped the average; he is, even
still, too great for their comprehension, too
wide and deep and brave a thinker for the
vulgar mediocrity of common and cringing
thought.

5. So fares the prophet on earth in matters
of religion. It is the same in matters of science.
At the beginning of the thirteenth century
after Christ a boy was born of a good family in
Somersetshire, who grew up to be one of the
greatest men whom the world has ever seen.
Only about once in a century does God kindle
the glory of an exceptional intellect; and,
alas! whenever such a light is kindled, the
world, which loves darkness, generally does its
best to quench it; even as, in some dim cave,
the birds which love the twilight will flap out
an uplifted torch with their obscure wings;
or as by night, in African wilds, the moths and

beetles will quench with their dark carcasses the traveller's lamp. This boy, born in 1214, was the founder of experimental philosophy. To him is due the very dawn of that science which is now the glory and blessing of the world. Even in that age, besides science, he mastered Greek, Latin, Hebrew, and Arabic. He was the earliest writer on chemistry in Europe. In his works he anticipated by three centuries the invention of the telescope; by four centuries the discovery of the laws of optics; by more than five centuries the invention of steam, suspension bridges, the diving bell, and the balloon. At that time what is called the scholastic system was triumphant. It was thought that there was no knowledge to be had outside the pages of Aristotle. For a Christian teacher to run counter to this heathen philosopher was to be a heretic. The student I speak of went to Oxford, and in order to devote his life to knowledge he became a Franciscan monk. He soon discovered that the Oxford of his day was languidly feeding on the thistles of a mere verbal knowledge; and that there was less to learn from all Aristotle, and all his commentators, than was to be learned from one line on the broad page of the works of God. He wrote a book which he called his "greater work" to show what were the chief causes of human ignorance. They were, he said, these four: (1) Servile deference to authority; (2) traditionary habit; (3) the neglect to train the senses to observe; and (4) the disposition to conceal our ignorance, and make a show of our supposed knowledge. Truer words were never uttered, and they are as applicable to religion as to science, and now as they were then. Now, what happened to this splendid benefactor of humanity among the hidebound slaves of pseudo-orthodox tradition? Ignorance, malignity, folly, and that sort of animal stupidity shown by men of decided opinions which are based on nothing—against which even the gods fight in vain—led the dull monks and stupid religionists of his day to accuse him of magic and sorcery. He spent thirty years of his life in prison. He was insulted, scorned, and, it is believed, even tortured. That man was Roger Bacon, a far greater man than Francis Bacon, Earl of Verulam, by whom his fame has been eclipsed. It was not till the age of seventy that, broken in heart and broken by suffering, he was liberated from prison. In the last eight years of his life he was able to do nothing. He was driven to the bitter thought that men, as he knew them, were so base, so little, and so ignorant that they were not worth the pain and toil which he had endured on their behalf. God had inbreathed an intellect into one of His children which would have anticipated by three centuries the richest blessings which science has bestowed upon mankind. God kindled it; man quenched it. Truly, " however we brazen it out, we men are a little breed." Had there been no persecuted prophets to be loftier than the common run of us, we should have been low indeed.

6. I give these two instances to show that a man may be a prophet in many directions, but that if we hope, if we try, in any direction to escape the average, it will cost us something. It may cost us nothing less than the success and happiness of our lives. So that I hope that not one will say, " What is all this to me? I cannot be a great religious thinker like Origen, or a great scientific discoverer like Roger Bacon. I cannot lift mankind from the slough of intellectual sloth and moral com-

promise in which they love to lie." Pardon me;
that is not quite true. We cannot be profound
and learned like Origen, or men of superb
genius like Roger Bacon, but every one of us
can be humble like Origen, and brave like
Origen, and unresentful like Origen ; and
candid, and thoughtful, and lovers of truth
like Roger Bacon; and we, like them both—in
great things or in little, as God shall grant
to us—may help to improve the moral judgments and to raise the moral standard of the
world. To do this requires no mental greatness, no grand position. It has been done
by youths and timid girls, by poor women
and penniless, persecuted men. Many a poor
woman or boy may think that what I have said
was not for them, because they never heard so
much as the names of these great men; well,
but their names, and the age in which they
lived, are of no consequence; what is of consequence is that they were just human beings,
who breathed common air of life, who had once
been little babes in the cradle as you and I
were. In our own way, to our own degree, we
can walk in their steps, as they walked in the
steps of their Saviour Christ.

7. For, mark, it does not want genius or power or learning to benefit men by braving their false judgments, by scorning their hypocritical alliances with sin, by opening their eyes to the infamy of accepted customs. It only wants—if I may use a vulgar word—it only wants pluck; fidelity; moral manliness. It wants no knowledge beyond that of the Lord's Prayer and the Ten Commandments in the vulgar tongue. It only wants the eyes open to see God's law. Yet how marvellously rare is this moral courage! Brute courage; instinctive courage; the courage of the tiger "which bounds with bare breast and unarmed claws upon the hunter's spear"; the flashy courage of the bully in the ring, or of the felon who, in his own brutal language, "wants to 'die game' upon the scaffold"—that is common enough; but the courage which dares to confront an angry king, or, standing up before a raging mob, dares to say, "You are wrong"; the courage which says, "I will not follow the multitude to do evil"; the courage which sees nothing but feebleness in the plea, "every one else does it, so I must do it too"; the courage of the man who, when standing up against

16

brute force for law and right, says, "No bullets and no threats shall cow me in the fulfilment of my plain duty"; still more the courage which can face and shame down a wrong custom amid the execrations of its votaries—*that* courage requires no genius except a moral genius which the most ignorant man or woman alive can show; and that moral genius of fearless rectitude is most astonishingly rare. We all know one memorable instance, to which I shall therefore but passingly allude. We know how, in ancient days, existed the horrible cruelty of public games in which criminals and gladiators—often barbarians—fought each other and stabbed each other to death before the yelling and gaping multitude. Who would have thought that such a custom would have survived no less than four centuries of Christianity? Yet it did; and we need not be so much surprised when we remember that our fathers looked on unmoved at the English brutalities of bear-baiting and cock-fighting; that dog-fighting still secretly survives; that there may be men even among my readers who have looked on at the foul and filthy spectacle of a prize-fight. But who stopped gladiatorial shows? Who wiped that infamy from the manners and morals of a nominally Christian Empire? Not emperors, or consuls, or lawyers, or writers of genius, or eloquent preachers, or learned divines, but just a rude, illiterate, unknown Asiatic monk, who had the courage to say, "This is wrong," and the courage to say, "So far as I am concerned it shall not be." The show was going on; the myriads were assembled in the Coliseum; the gladiators were matched; the Emperor was in the chair; there was a clash of swords and a stream of blood, and the horrible spectacle had fairly begun. Then, in his monk's rude dress, down into the arena leaped the intrepid man, and, unarmed as he was, thrust himself between the weapons of that murderous struggle. It was the poor unknown monk Telemachus. "Who is he? What presumptuous insolence! Down with him!" The mob hooted, yelled, raged, leaped over the barriers, hurled stones at him, would have rent him limb from limb. The very gladiators whom he would have saved turned their swords against him. He fell a mangled mass, beaten to death by innumerable blows. It is the only day of all his life of which a single fact is known. But

what a day! it was a day in which his plain
sense of right and wrong, his plain courage in
acting up to it, had done nothing less than
liberate the world!

> Sound, sound the trumpet; shrill the fife!
>   To all the sensual world proclaim,
> One crowded hour of glorious life
>   Is worth a world without a name!

8. Let me give another instance. It requires
no small courage to resist the power and decrees
of kings. It is never right to do so except when
righteousness and truth demand, and one is
sorry to see those high clear issues confused for
the sake of mere fantastic puerilities. When
they do, when there is a clear collision between
conscience and the civil power, no good man,
no true man, no brave man, ought to flinch.
Isaiah, we see, did not flinch before Ahaz and
Manasseh; nor Elijah before Jezebel; nor St.
Ambrose before Theodosius; nor St. Chrysos-
tom before Eudoxia. Yet even Luther and
Melancthon did before Philip of Hesse. John
had said to Herod, with noble and blunt
forthrightness, "It is not lawful for thee to
have her"; yet Luther and Melancthon —
though the shame of it afterwards almost broke

Melancthon's heart—practically allowed Philip of Hesse to contract a bigamous marriage. Now *we*, thank God, are never likely, in any worthy or sensible cause, to come into collision with the civil power; but there is not one of us who may not have to confront some superior— our employer in an office, our master in a shop, if they bid us do wrong. And this may cost us much; and there is a tremendous temptation not to do it. Yet how invaluable to others one brave word, one brave act, may be! In the reign of James II., in 1683, the clergy were ordered to read a declaration which they held to be illegal. Even eminent laymen advised submission; and to refuse it was to brave a tyrant as unscrupulous and as cruel as he was narrow and bigoted. Bishop Sprat had the baseness to comply, and with pale face and shaking hands he read it in the Abbey amid the noise of the congregation as they indignantly crowded out. But fifteen London clergymen met to consider whether they should do it. They were inclined to yield, when Dr. Edward Fowler got up and said, " I must be plain. The question is quite simple. Let each man say yes or no. But I cannot be bound by the

vote even of the majority. This declaration I
cannot in conscience read." His courage fired
the rest, carried the day, and saved England
from a Popish tyranny. In four churches, only,
of London was the order read. The father of
John Wesley, then a curate in London, chose for
his text that day the words, " Be it known unto
thee, O King, that we will not serve thy gods,
nor worship the golden image which thou hast
set up."

9. This is to act in the spirit of a prophet.
It is to see the truth plainly, and to act up to
it boldly; to see the truth unblinded by the
mists of self-interest or the cobwebs of casuistry;
to act up to it though rulers may threaten and
mobs may yell.

I will give another illustration in our own
day. In the youth of many of us duels were
still common. The statesman of that time, the
literary men of that time, had—many of them
—been engaged in duels, as some living men
of eminence have been. The custom was bad,
as un-Christian, as anti-Christian as anything
could be; it was " a mixture of fashion and
revengefulness, of murder and suicide." And
yet society, so far from condemning it, consi-

dered it a necessary institution; and every
hot-blooded young fool who misunderstood a
neighbour's remark thought himself entitled to
demand what he called " satisfaction." Now,
though this spirit of murderous resentment and
this reckless disregard of human life stood
utterly condemned before the bar of every
moral law, it required a very brave man indeed
to resist it. A story is told of one such brave
man. An insulting adversary spat in his face.
" Young man," he said, " if I could wipe your
blood off my conscience as easily as I can wipe
your insult off my face, I would strike you dead
this moment." But the person who did more
than any one to give the death-blow to this
wicked and senseless custom in our day was a
peer—the Earl of Shaftesbury—who stands
foremost for his services to mankind. Years
ago he received a challenge from some bluster-
ing opponent. Instead of accepting it, he wrote
back a quietly contemptuous refusal, and sent
the letters to the police-court and the newspapers. After that the proposal to settle a
quarrel by being shot at and shooting at some
one else—a mode of settlement which, though it
did not stand above the level of the morality of

the Ojibways, yet, simply because it was the custom of society, did not strike our grand-fathers as grotesque or wrong—fell before the force of courage and insight into moral contempt and merited disgrace.

I have dwelt on these instances solely because the concrete is more likely to explain itself, more likely to act as a motive, than the abstract. And, not to talk only of distant and heroic things and persons of which history tells, I will give a very modern and every-day instance. The story has got into books; it has been told of various schools and other communities, but, as I tell it you, it was told me by one who knew, and was himself an actor in the scene. More than forty years ago, at a great English school (and in those days that state of things was common), no boy in the large dormitories ever dared to say his prayers. A young new boy—neither strong, nor distinguished, nor brilliant, nor influential, nor of high rank—came to the school. The first night that he slept in his dormitory not one boy knelt to say his prayers. But the new boy knelt down as he had always done. He was jeered at, insulted, pelted, kicked for it;

and so he was the next night, and the next.
But after a night or two, not only did the
persecution cease, but another boy knelt down
as well as himself, and then another, until it
became the custom for every boy to kneel
nightly at the altar of his own bed side. From
that dormitory, in which my informant was,
the custom spread to other dormitories, one
by one. When that young new boy came to
the school no boy said his prayers; when he
left it, without one act or word on his part beyond the silent influence of a quiet and brave
example, *all* the boys said their prayers. The
right act had prevailed against the bad custom and the blinded cowardice of that little
world. That boy still lives; and if he had
never done one good deed besides that deed,
be sure it stands written for him in golden
letters in the Recording Angel's book. Now,
is not that kind of act an act which any one
of us, from the richest statesman down to the
youngest boy, might imitate? Are there no bad
customs, no immoral conventions, no base ac-
quiescences, no tolerated evils, in society? And
if so, have you no share in them? Have you
made no attempt to make a compromise be-

17

tween Christ and Belial? Are there no temples
of Rimmon in England? And, if so, have
we never bowed in them? Well, whenever we
see a wrong deed and have the courage to
say, "It is wrong, and I, for one, will have
nothing to do with it"; whenever we come
in contact with a low and un-Christian standard,
or a bad, unworthy habit, and are men enough
first to refuse for our own part to succumb to it, and then to do our best to overthrow it—we are prophets. Indeed, those
who live in poor streets have even more oppor-
tunities of taking this line and of making this
stand than others have. If the Gospel means
the example of our Lord Jesus Christ, remember that this is the Gospel and nothing but the
Gospel, though it be not expressed in the shibboleths which Pharisees are most fond of writing on their broad phylacteries. For this—to
see sin, which tried to pass itself off for virtue;
to expose hypocrisy, which wore the garb of
religion; to save society which was perishing
of its own hidden corruption; to teach truth,
though men hated it; to scatter darkness,
though men loved it; to reveal the God of
Love, though men had represented Him as a

Moloch of hatred; to teach men that their work in life was to love and to help their fellow-men, and so (and not by mere exclusive formulæ and malignant orthodoxies) to save their own souls—this, this emphatically, was the work of Christ:—*His* work and therefore our work, for which He will inspire the courage. Be brave, be just, be truthful and honest to the heart's core, and so serve your brother man, and so serve best your Father God, and your Saviour the Lord Christ. If those be not lessons of the Gospel of the Pharisees, they are—ten thousandfold more than a gloomy Calvinism or a sectarian shib-boleth—the lessons of the Gospel of Christ. "There are," a great statesman said, "there are steeps of Alma on the field of duty no less than on the field of blood." The question is, will we be one of the vulgar throng that will not face them, or will we be individual soldiers, however humble, in the "thin red line" that carries them against the foe? If of the latter, then God will make us, too, His prophets, and will say to us, as to Ezekiel:

"And thou, son of man, be not afraid of

them. Be not afraid of their faces; be not afraid of their words, though briers and thorns be with thee, and thou dost dwell among scorpions."

THE END.

W. S____ ht & Sons, Printers, Fetter Lane, London.